"*Joined by the Church, Sealed by a Bl* parishes who desire to revitalize sacra are preparing for the Sacrament of Ma challenges and inspired by the baptismal catechumenate, the authors present a new approach to marriage ministry focused on conversion and lifelong discipleship. The book outlines a formation process that engages the couple in a deeper life of faith and calls the entire community of faith to accompany them on the journey. Like the RCIA, this new approach to marriage sacramental ministry has the possibility of transforming the entire parish community through marriage preparation, celebration, and ongoing pastoral ministry with couples. If you are hoping to inspire young couples and your parish community to a deeper, living faith, you will find great inspiration in this book!"

Karen Kane
Director of Worship
Archdiocese of Cincinnati

"A wedding that celebrates the conversion process of a man and woman like the Easter vigil does for the catechumenate? Could that be? In *Joined by the Church, Sealed by a Blessing*, Macalintal and Wagner propose a fresh vision for marriage preparation that parallels the RCIA process: a call to discipleship formed within a parish community that nurtures neophyte families. Pastors and parish leaders—if your marriage prep isn't 'working' to create committed Christian couples, this book offers practical pathways to rethink, restructure, and breathe new life into your process."

Karla J. Bellinger, DMin, author of *Connecting Pulpit and Pew*, director of the Center for Preaching, Evangelization, and Prayer

Joined by the Church, Sealed by a Blessing

Couples and Communities Called to Conversion Together

Diana Macalintal and Nick Wagner

LITURGICAL PRESS

Collegeville, Minnesota

www.litpress.org

Nihil Obstat: Reverend Robert Harren, *Censor deputatus.*

Imprimatur: ✠ Most Reverend Donald J. Kettler, J.C.L., Bishop of Saint Cloud, Minnesota. May 22, 2014.

Cover design by Stefan Killen Design. Photograph by Debbie Winarski, © 2012. Blessing of the bride and groom, Kate and Scott Williams, on October 20, 2012, by the community of Saint Nicholas Church in Evanston, Illinois.

Excerpts from documents of the Second Vatican Council are from *Vatican Council II: The Basic Sixteen Documents*, by Austin Flannery, OP © 1996 (Costello Publishing Company, Inc.). Used with permission.

Excerpts from the English translation of *Order of Celebrating Marriage* (Second Typical Edition) © 1996 (provisional text), International Commission on English in the Liturgy Corporation (ICEL). Excerpts from the English translation of *Rite of Christian Initiation of Adults* © 1985, ICEL. All rights reserved.

Scripture texts, prefaces, introductions, footnotes and cross references used in this work are taken from the *New American Bible, revised edition* © 2010, 1991, 1986, 1970 Confraternity of Christian Doctrine, Washington, DC and are used by permission of the copyright owner. All Rights Reserved. No part of the New American Bible may be reproduced in any form without permission in writing from the copyright owner.

"Coffee Hour Caution" on page 28 © Office of Youth and Young Adult Ministries, Unitarian Universalist Association, uua.org/youngadults. Reprinted with permission.

1   2   3   4   5   6   7   8   9

Library of Congress Cataloging-in-Publication Data

Macalintal, Diana.
   Joined by the church, sealed by a blessing : couples and communities
called to conversion together / Diana Macalintal and Nick Wagner.
      pages   cm
   ISBN 978-0-8146-3765-4 — ISBN 978-0-8146-3790-6 (ebook)
   1. Marriage—Religious aspects—Catholic Church.   2. Church membership.
   3. Spiritual formation—Catholic Church.   4. Conversion—Catholic Church.
   5. Church group work—Catholic Church.   I. Title.
   BX2250.M128   2014
   261.8'3581—dc23   2014007737

How can I ever express the happiness of the marriage that is
joined together by the Church,
strengthened by an offering,
sealed by a blessing,
announced by angels,
and ratified by the Father?

—Tertullian (160–220 AD),
in a letter to his wife

Contents

1

Stop Preparing for Marriage;
Start Preparing for Discipleship

There are a lot of reasons to get discouraged when you think about helping couples prepare for marriage in the Catholic Church. Beyond the weird stories about unusual liturgical requests, the frustrating stories about demanding couples, and the sad stories about broken families, there is a bigger story. This story is about not only our changing social values but also the inadequate state of our parishes to meet those changing needs. You know these stories. They're happening right in your own parish.

Joe and Karen Become a Statistic

Joe and Karen are your typical "middle-pew" parishioners. They come to Mass more regularly than most young adults, but that's the extent of their participation in the parish. They were married at this same parish last June, and they're now expecting their first child. The parish staff had led them through the basic marriage preparation process and had even added a couple of special blessings for them at Mass during their engagement. The liturgical staff had made sure their wedding was not only beautiful but also followed good liturgical principles, and the couple's families and friends were impressed. On top of all that, the pastor had sent them a note one month after the wedding with continued prayers for a happy marriage. This parish puts a priority on building strong Catholic families, and so they invest a lot of time, money, creativity, and resources into preparing the engaged couples who come to them. Everyone seems happy . . . until Joe loses his job, and Karen's father moves in with them after his stroke. Over the next couple of years, the strain on their relationship and the long nights fighting cause them to come to Mass less and less often. One Sunday, Karen shows up by herself, sitting in the back pew with her toddler.

Joe and Karen have become one of the 40 to 50 percent of marriages in the United States that end in divorce. Even for people like them, who marry in the church and are relatively active in their faith, they still only have a slightly better chance at not getting divorced than their nonreligious, civilly married friends.[1]

More Time with the Grandkids but Less Money for the Budget

Josefina prides herself at the care she takes in helping wedding couples on their big day. She's been coordinating weddings at her parish for almost ten years, and couples say she's the best. She doesn't mind spending all of her Friday evenings and Saturday mornings at the church, running rehearsals and being there for the weddings. However, lately, she finds that she has a lot more free time, since there aren't as many weddings being scheduled on the parish calendar. She's not upset because it gives her more time to spend with her grandkids. However, it does worry the pastor, who sees a lot more people in long-term committed relationships choosing not to get married. How can he help them understand the value and dignity of Christian marriage in today's society? And the parish bookkeeper is also anxious because of this drop in the number of weddings. That's because fewer weddings also means less money coming in to pay not only for Josefina's part-time salary but also for basic maintenance of the parish facilities.

Wedding coordinators across the country are getting more free time, and pastors and bookkeepers are getting more ulcers because since 1972, the number of church weddings in the US Catholic Church has dropped 60 percent.[2] Today, fewer people overall are deciding to get married, and if they do, they're more likely to choose a destination wedding at a beach resort rather than their neighborhood parish.

The New Normal

At Father George's church, the parish bulletin shows the total Sunday collection from the previous week, and it's hard for anyone not to notice the slow and steady decline in donations. Father George wonders if he's doing something wrong since he became the new pastor a year ago. He works hard at his homilies and tries to be as welcoming as possible, going early to every Mass and staying long after to greet his parishioners. He's already married dozens of couples and baptized a bunch more babies in the parish, but he hasn't seen any of them back in the church. His staff and parishioners he's grown close to reassure him that he's doing a great job and he shouldn't worry. But empty pews don't lie. He may be a good pastor, but the people just aren't there to see it.

Father George is encountering the new normal in the church—Catholics who come to church only for Christmas and Easter or weddings and funerals. In 2012, less than 20 percent of US adult Catholics attended Mass once a week or more, aside from weddings and funerals.[3] This isn't simply a case of parishioners having too many things to do and not enough time for Mass. Many younger people along with their parents believe that going to Sunday Mass is not necessary to be a good Catholic. They will be many of your newlyweds whom you won't see again until Christmas or when it's time for their babies' baptisms or their parents' funerals.

The Really Scary Part of This Story

Now imagine your church filled with your parishioners. See their faces, those who have been there for years before you even got there and those you barely recognize. Now remove 75 percent of those parishioners from your pews. That's how many people you might lose in the next five years to the fastest-growing denomination in the US—the "nones." Almost three-quarters of people who self-identify as practicing no particular faith or religion are people who *used to be* part of a church.[4] Most of us don't see the dramatic shift in our parish numbers because of the growth of Hispanic and Asian Catholics in the US. Their presence is certainly a blessing, but it also brings its own unique challenges as well. If you're not yet aware of wedding traditions such as the giving and receiving of *arras*, the use of the veil and cord, the multitude of sponsors, or the honoring of ancestors, then you'll need to start learning.

There Can Be a "Happily Ever After"

These four stories and their challenges are indeed daunting and can be upsetting. But we wrote this book to help you and your parish face these challenges with confidence, creativity, and clarity. Other resources can help you plan excellent wedding celebrations and prepare couples well for a lifetime commitment. We'll also try to help you do that. However, what we hope that this book really helps you with is another C word—conversion.

What is at the heart of the preparation processes in this resource is the centrality of conversion to Christ. Certainly this conversion has to take place within the couples themselves. In their vocation of marriage, they will live out this conversion primarily in their dying to self for the sake of their spouses and children. Their preparation for marriage, then, needs to be an apprenticeship in this kind of joyful, sacrificial way of life for the other.

However, the couples are not the only place where conversion needs to happen. Their entire preparation for marriage touches the lives of so many of their own loved ones, friends, family, and even casual acquaintances who journey with them through their engagement and beyond. The couples and the parish that helps to prepare them have an opportunity to share moments of conversion with all these people in big and small ways. Their preparation for marriage, then, also needs to help them and the parish become "evangelizers" for the source of their love, who is Christ.

Now here's the kicker. For any of this to actually happen, conversion needs to begin with the parish, not the couples. Your parishioners are your most influential resource. They will be the reason your newlyweds decide to stay as parishioners. The parishioners will be the people newlyweds look to when they hit rough ground in those early days of married life. As imperfect as they are, and perhaps even because of it, parishioners are your best resource for helping couples learn what it means to live a life of faith and commitment in community together—because that's what they are.

Your job then is to guide your wedding couples on a journey of conversion by letting your parish and the people in it be the place where that conversion can happen.

A Successful Conversion Model in Four Steps

The best process the church has for drawing people to deeper conversion to Christ is the catechumenate, or the Rite of Christian Initiation of Adults (RCIA). The goal of the catechumenate is to bring "the faithful of Christ, to his full stature and to enable [them] to carry out the mission of the entire people of God in the Church and in the world" (Christian Initiation, General Introduction, 2).

1. Evangelization

The way the catechumenate does this is by calling the church to do what it exists to do: to evangelize.[5] By their very actions and words, your parishioners are called to "faithfully and constantly" proclaim the living God (RCIA, 36). When your engaged couples—and those thinking about getting engaged—encounter that living God through the words and actions of the parishioners they meet, there is an opportunity for conversion. Only then can true and honest formation into this vocation begin.

2. Formation

In their period of preparation for married life, your wedding couples are mentored by the parish in living out the paschal mystery by

- reflecting on and studying the word of God;
- immersing themselves into the life and mission of the community;
- praying and worshiping within the assembly and at home;
- serving others in ways that proclaim the living God in our midst.

3. Spiritual Preparation

During the weeks before their wedding, these engaged couples, having been apprenticed in this new vocation, prepare more intensely for their marriage through spiritual disciplines and deepened reflection on the marriage rite.

4. Mystagogical Reflection

Then, in the days, months, and years after the wedding, the parish continues to journey with these newlyweds as they break open the experience of the wedding liturgy and live out its meaning in their daily lives.

An engaged couple's journey to married life is a gradual process that takes place in and with the community. Their progress is marked and strengthened by rituals, prayers, and blessings that lead them into deeper conversion to the dying and rising of Christ. The goal of this process is not simply marriage but mature, intentional faith lived out in the vocation and mission of married life. Most of all, this process is not a one-size-fits-all preparation. Each couple will have unique needs and challenges. Each couple will come to you at a different place in their life of faith than the next couple and the one before. You and your preparation process need to be flexible enough and creative enough to meet each couple's specific needs while working with the resources you have at hand.

This kind of wedding preparation process is shaped after the basic structure and primary characteristics of the catechumenate. By using the RCIA as our model and inspiration, without slavishly reinterpreting its process for wedding couples, we can benefit from its power, comprehensiveness, and simplicity. Most of all, you will find that when you begin with conversion as the goal, not only will your wedding couples be transformed, but so will your parish.

Who Is This Resource For?

Because this preparation process is modeled after the catechumenate, which sees the formation of adults into Christian faith as "the responsibility of all the baptized" (RCIA, 9), this resource is written specifically for the Catholic parish and its leaders.

The Four Challenges

Pastors and pastoral leaders will find this resource most beneficial since it strives to address the four challenges that began this chapter:

1. Increased divorce rates even among Christians

2. Fewer Catholic weddings

3. Empty pews on Sundays

4. More people simply choosing no faith

These challenges cannot be solved overnight by any plan, as comprehensive as it might be. Yet if we go by our own experience of those who have been initiated into the church through the catechumenate, we know that this kind of conversion-based process creates more passionate and engaged Christians. This marriage preparation plan, like the RCIA process, is certainly not foolproof. But it does give you a better way of doing what the Order of Celebrating Marriage asks when it says that "pastors are to welcome engaged couples and, above all, they are to foster and nourish their faith: for the Sacrament of Matrimony presupposes and demands faith" (16).

Rethink Your Team

Your wedding preparation team, of course, will also be enriched and challenged by this resource. However, this team may be bigger than you think. We will say a lot more about who is on your team in chapter 11. For now, keep these insights in mind.

Parishioners

The first and most valuable members of your team will be your parishioners. So this preparation process will challenge you to look differently at how your current process can be more integrated into the life of the parish. It will challenge you to look at the activities of your parish to see where formation for married life can happen outside of the classroom, meeting hall, or parish office. And it will call you to find "mentors" from among your everyday parishioners who can serve as guides and support for your engaged couples.

Liturgy Team

Next, this resource will give your marriage preparation coordinator, your wedding liturgy coordinator, your parish musician, and those who typically assist at your wedding liturgies guidance on how to make what they already do part of the conversion process of these couples and their families and friends. These meetings and moments that are focused on the wedding liturgy are golden opportunities to touch the hearts of not just the couple but more importantly the hundreds of family members and friends they bring to the church with them on their big day. Yet we too often miss these opportunities because we get so caught up on the couple alone. Your pastoral and liturgical staff needs to focus on preparing conversion moments for those forgotten hundreds as well. We will give you simple ways to do just that.

Parish Staff

Finally, your wedding preparation team includes others on your parish staff. So this book will give ideas for your parish receptionist or secretary, who often is your parish's first contact with couples. For better or worse, this person sets the tone for your entire process. Next, your adult faith formation coordinator or director of religious education (DRE) will also find guidance here on how to collaborate better with the marriage preparation team so that the faith of your couples is systematically and completely nourished and strengthened. At times, you will also need to enlist the help of your RCIA and confirmation coordinators, since many engaged couples may also be seeking to celebrate the sacraments of initiation or to be received into the communion of the Catholic Church. These couples will need a specialized plan that integrates their marriage and initiation preparation while acknowledging that both processes are unique.

How to Use This Resource

This book is more than just another marriage preparation resource. It's a parish transformation tool. In this book, you will discover:

- How to connect the liturgy to people's daily lives
- Why people come to (and stay at) a parish
- How to preach the Gospel without being preachy about it
- Best practices for parish leaders to transform their parish into a place where people can thrive in their faith so as to live it out in their lives

Take Small Steps

That's a lot of stuff crammed into these pages. But ultimately, we want you to know how to make your wedding preparation process the best it can be. Doing that will not be easy; it may require you and your parish to make some changes. Yet making the choice to try is simple. So don't get overwhelmed by the scope of this process. If the ideal goal is too big to even think about right now, then just decide to make one small change this year and another small change next year. Let your goals be achievable yet still challenging. Mark your successes, and make your shortfalls opportunities for learning.

If you don't have time to read the entire book right now, just pick the parts that you need most, and just read those chapters for now. We divided this book into parts that can be used independently.

What's Inside

Chapters 2, 3, and 4 go more in-depth into the catechumenate process, what it does to change people's fundamental outlook on the purpose of their faith, and how it does that. Too often, engaged couples see the marriage preparation process at their parish as simply more hoops to go through in order to have the wedding of their dreams. Here, we'll give you a method for helping them deepen their faith and connection to the church so they can live the marriage that God has prepared for them. If you want a good understanding of the principles of conversion and the parish's role in preparing opportunities for conversion, then don't skip these chapters. If you can get a solid understanding of these principles, you will be able to use them to transform any liturgy and preparation process your parish does—weddings, funerals, First Communion, confirmation, penance—to make them more powerful ways for your entire parish to draw visitors, first-timers, and marginal Catholics into a deeper life of faith.

Chapter 5 gives you an overview of the stages of marriage preparation, and chapters 5 through 8 show you step-by-step how to lead couples through each of those stages.

In chapter 9, we give you some ways to help couples engage in the practice of discernment. Most of them already know and believe they are ready for marriage. Yet discernment is more than just about knowing if you're ready; it's about learning to listen deeply to the Spirit throughout our entire lives. We'll give you ways to help these couples learn to follow the Spirit's lead in all the significant decisions they will make together.

Chapter 10 gives you practical ways to ritualize the various stages of the couples' preparation, and it provides prayers you can give to them to use at home. This helps them, if they have not already, begin to integrate prayer into their daily lives so that their homes can truly be the domestic church that sustains their participation in the parish church.

Chapter 11 helps you develop a comprehensive team that is integrated into the entire parish's efforts at hospitality, sacramental preparation, adult faith formation, and liturgy. Chapter 12 gives you some help with the difficult issues that will certainly arise, such as annulments, mixed-faith marriages, pregnancy before marriage, difficult family situations, and couples who are indifferent to the Christian way of life.

The last chapter moves us back to the bigger picture, asking ourselves, "What if?" What if we really did marriage prep like this in our parish? How would it change us? How would it change our couples? How will Christ be more known to the world because of what we have done here? When we keep these big-picture questions in mind, we will be doing more than just preparing couples for their big day. We'll be doing the mission of Christ to transform the world in which we live.

2

Why Is Conversion Important?

Job One: Conversion

Now, you probably picked up this book because you thought we'll tell you how to improve your marriage preparation process and get your couples married. Well, what if we told you that getting married isn't the point?

The most important point of the initiation process is that it's all about conversion to Christ.

It's also the most important point for Christian marriage preparation. Couples come to us at different levels of conversion. Often, the couples we are working with have little or no faith. Or their faith is in a flawed image of an impersonal, distant God. If we are truly preparing couples for a sacramental marriage, we have to evangelize them to sure and mature faith in the risen Christ.

In the catechumenate, the goal of formation is not baptism; it is conversion, that is,

- transformation of a person from having no faith to having faith in Christ;
- from feeling despair caused by suffering to being hopeful even in the face of death;
- from seeing oneself as an individual to knowing intimately that we are bound to one another, especially to those most in need, because we are all children of God.

Conversion is the goal; baptism is the outcome—the result—of this gradual and ongoing conversion to Christ, and it completes and strengthens that total change of life.

Preparation for marriage should be seen in the same way. The goal is not to get married. The goal is to strengthen one's conversion of heart toward the attitudes, skills, and knowledge necessary for living one's faith in Christ through the Christian vocation of marriage. What are the conversion points for married life, and how can we make marriage preparation a more conversion-oriented process?

Setting Conversion Goals

Here is a sacramental secret. If you want to know what to catechize about in preparation for a sacrament, look at the liturgy. Specifically, look for the questions that get asked in the liturgy. In the Order of Celebrating Marriage (OCM), the bride and groom each answer specific questions before making the marriage vows. These questions and responses serve as the final public confirmation of that person's readiness to enter into the sacrament he or she is about to celebrate. The church takes these questions so seriously that you could actually structure your entire marriage preparation process around these three questions alone, and you would basically cover the entirety of what we understand to be Christian marriage.

Let's take a look at each of these questions and what conversion movements we need to look for based on each question. Note that although the minister asks these questions of the bride and groom together, each one responds separately.

Free Will

> N. and N., *have you come here to enter into Marriage without coercion,*
> *freely and wholeheartedly?* (OCM, 60)

A basic theological principle that we see here in the ritual is the principle of free will. God does not force any of his creatures to love him but constantly offers the gift of grace, his presence, to those who choose to accept it.

Although Great-Aunt Sally might regale everyone about her own "shotgun wedding" to Great-Uncle Max, in a true Christian sense, no one can be forced into marriage. There may be circumstances that make getting married a more urgent matter. A person might feel pressure from parents, friends, societal norms, his or her partner, perhaps even one's own physical or mental condition. Maybe he or she is just afraid of being alone.

Yet, all individuals must make this choice for themselves, apart from these pressures, understanding the responsibility they take by that choice, and being fully accountable for the making of that choice regardless of the circumstances involved. They must also be intellectually and legally capable of making this choice for themselves. Further, they make this choice not because it's the "logical" choice to make; they make it with their whole heart.

Jessica grew up with "helicopter parents," those who hovered over her constantly, directing her choices and decisions. They did this out of love and concern for her well-being. But it also kept her from learning how to discern her own needs.

Joseph always believed he'd marry someone from his own Vietnamese culture. That's just what his family expects of him and what all of his siblings and cousins have done. What is he going to do now that he's fallen in love with Carmen from Mexico?

For many couples, especially younger couples, having a significant relationship is often one of the first adult, independent actions they take apart from their parents. However, age is not always a marker for maturity, nor does it give us a sense of a person's independence and autonomy. So what we're looking for here is a conversion in mind and heart from conformity, manipulation, and fear to a sense of liberty, openness, and peace.

As part of their preparation, you might invite your couples to discern their progress in this conversion by having them reflect on this first question from the rite. They might journal individually, and then share together their responses to these reflection questions:

- Who or what have been the major influences in my life? How have those persons or things influenced me in making this decision to get married?
- How have I made significant decisions in the past? Have I been happy with the major decisions I have made so far?

(The following might be asked at various points throughout the process to discern if there has been any change in heart or new insight.)

- Why is getting married the right decision for me to make at this time in my life?
- If I chose not to get married now, what would happen? Am I afraid of disappointing anyone?
- Am I afraid of whatever consequences I think might happen if I did not get married now?
- If my partner chose not to marry me now, what would happen? Am I open to accepting that decision?

As they share their responses, you might place their discussion into a Christian context by including Scripture passages that point to God's invitation and our free will to follow, for example, Luke 1:26-38; John 1:35-46; Galatians 5:1; 2 Corinthians 3:17-18. Also, introducing them to some of the spiritual exercises of St. Ignatius might also be helpful for them in finding peace in their decision-making process. (See chapter 9 for some ideas.)

Commitment

> *Are you prepared, as you follow the path of Marriage,*
> *to love and honor each other*
> *for as long as you both shall live?* (OCM, 60)

In weddings, we tend to focus a lot on the aspect of love. (When have you *not* heard "Love is patient, love is kind . . . " at a Christian wedding? Somewhere along the line, engaged couples somehow got some fake memo telling them this was a required reading if they wanted to get married in the church.)

This question from the marriage rite gives us a broader under-standing of what Christian marriage is. First, it's a path. The English text translates the Latin word *viam*, which also means "way." In the Acts of the Apostles, the first Christians were called the people who belonged to "the Way." You knew who were followers of Jesus because of the way of life they lived. In marriage, we become people who live "the way" of marriage. Marriage, in this sense, is much more a verb than it is a noun. It is a way of loving and honoring one another all along the path of life.

So one conversion marker we need to look for here is the movement from understanding marriage as a *state* in life—an event, a day—to marriage as a *way* of life. As with any path, the terrain and conditions may change. A snarky comedian once asked why a woman works ten years to change a man's habits and then complains that he's not the man she married. But it's true! None of us wind up with the exact person we married. Each of us changes, and so do our relationships. The way we love and honor one another might look very different ten, twenty, thirty years down the path than it does now at this stage in life. Yet the commitment to staying on the path and the mission of the path (to love and honor one another) does not change.

The second point we find in this ritual question reminds us that loving and honoring another person is not a feeling but a choice we should be prepared to make each day along the path. Some marriage retreat programs use the motto, "Love is a choice," and they're right. Taking on the vocation of marriage means that one chooses to love and honor the other even if he or she doesn't feel like it. It is the responsibility and duty that comes with this vocation; it is the role of one who is a member of the order of married persons.

Therefore, another conversion marker to watch for is the movement from depending on the feelings of love to sustain the relationship to depending on the promise that is made.

Promise

In act 2 of his play *The Skin of Our Teeth* (1942), American playwright Thornton Wilder says this of the powerful, overwhelming strength of a promise:

> I didn't marry you because you were perfect. I didn't even marry you because I loved you. I married you because you gave me a promise. That promise made up for your faults. And the promise I gave you made up for mine. Two imperfect people got married, and it was the promise that made the marriage. . . . And when our children were growing up, it wasn't a house that protected them; and it wasn't our love that protected them—it was that promise.

Some journal questions you might use to help them reflect on this promise in the rite are

- What do I think are the differences between marriage as an event and marriage as a way of life?
  - Describe what a couple does and says who sees marriage as an event.
  - Describe what a couple does and says who sees marriage as a way of life.
- What do I imagine being married will be like ten, twenty, thirty years from now?
- Who in my life are models for me of people who live the "way of marriage"?
  - Am I a person who keeps my promises? What can I do, in big and small ways, to be a person who lives by my word?
  - What is my reaction when someone breaks a promise to me? Can I keep my promises even if I have been hurt?

Consider incorporating some of our Christian teaching and tradition into the discussion, such as,

- the power of God's Word; Christ, the Logos, the Word made flesh;
- the "performative" word of sacraments, that is, the words we say in ritual make real what we intend by those words;
- the witness of long-married couples or religious in professed life;
- the story of Mother Teresa and her faithfulness even when she might have felt empty of faith ("God has not called me to be successful; He has called me to be faithful").

Doubts

At a gathering with schoolchildren and their parents and teachers, Pope Francis decided to skip his prepared talk and simply answer questions from the audience. One of the older boys admitted to the pope that he often had doubts about his own faith and asked the pope what he should do in those times of doubt. The pope responded, "There are days of darkness and some days of falls, one falls, falls. But always think this, don't be afraid of the failures, don't be afraid of the falls. . . . Don't be afraid of falling, in the art of falling what is important isn't not falling, but not remaining down" (Estefania Aguirre, "Pope gives children advice on facing doubts about faith," *Catholic News Agency*, June 7, 2013, http://www.catholicnewsagency.com /news/pope-tells-children-how-to-face-doubts-about-faith/).

Fruitfulness

> *Are you prepared to accept children lovingly from God
> and to bring them up
> according to the law of Christ and his Church?* (OCM, 60)

The rite gives the minister the option to omit this question if the circumstances seem to call for it, as in the case with elderly couples. There may be a need to make use of this option; but there may also be another way to look at this question that goes beyond simply the ability of the couple to procreate.

Sometimes in the church's history, married persons seemed to hold second-class status in holiness among the people of God. If you wanted to be really holy, you had to be a virgin and stay that way. Therefore, those professed to the religious or ordained vocations were seen as holier than Mr. and Mrs. Smith down the block whose gaggle of children raised a ruckus every Sunday at Mass. Now, if a person still decided to choose the less-than-holy way of life, in the church's thinking at that time, there had to be some beneficial reason for doing so. Therefore, the church stated that the main reason to get married was to have and raise children in the Christian faith. Love, mutual support, and—if you *had* to have them—the controlling of sexual desires came second (see 1917 Code of Canon Law, c. 1013.1).

The Second Vatican Council changed all that and taught that marriage is *another way* to holiness in which a man and woman "increasingly further their own perfection and their mutual sanctification, and together they render glory to God" (Pastoral Constitution on the Church in the Modern World, 48).[1] Now, equal importance is given to this vocation and way of holiness in which the complete handing over of oneself to another person in love is given the same worth as having children (see OCM, 8). Thus, giving one's life to a spouse as well as to children are both ways of being fruitful in a marriage. This self-sacrifice, whether to each other or to their children, is the foundation of the "mission" of marriage. Just as Jesus gave himself over for the life of the world, so too do all the baptized who are his disciples. In a special way, married persons sacrifice themselves for the life of the one they marry and most especially for their children and those they care for in their home. By their words and actions, they preach the Gospel. In their witness of the Christian faith, they draw others into that faith and nurture them by their way of life. Like priests whose role is above all "to help the individual discover his personal vocation" (Pope Benedict XVI),[2] they help each other, their own children, and those they meet to discern and follow the unique path that God has set before each one of them.

The Sacrifice

"We use language about conversion and paschal mystery in speaking about the reality of married love—and about mutual and lasting fidelity as a witness to God's steadfast love—because these realities need to be spoken to a starry-eyed couple caught up in the easy springtime of relationship, where life abounds and death in its many guises seems remote. Until couples face up to and embrace the real demands of conversion, until they choose to die as well as to love—and to beg God's help and God's blessing on all their loving and all their dying—their marriage has not yet become a sacrament. A wedding does not make a marriage. A wedding simply makes a marriage possible" (Kathleen Hughes, *Saying Amen: A Mystagogy of Sacrament* [Chicago: Liturgy Training Publications, 1999], 106).

Domestic Church

Marriage is more than two people. Most couples know this, but sometimes they don't think about it clearly enough. Most engaged couples will become parents (if they are not already!). We need to help them realize that their marriage extends beyond themselves to their family. Even childless couples have a responsibility to others beyond themselves.

The bishops at the Second Vatican Council said this of families:

> In what might be regarded as the domestic church, the parents are to be the first preachers of the faith for their children by word and example. They must foster the vocation which is proper to each child, taking special care if it be a sacred vocation. (Dogmatic Constitution on the Church, 11)

Married couples are called to make their homes like church—a holy place. In that domestic church, just as in the parish church, they nourish and strengthen their family community so that they may go out each day into the world to sanctify it by their lives.

This third question in the rite ultimately examines couples' readiness for the mission of marriage—to bless the world with their love through their own lives and, if God has called them to be parents, through their children, whether biological or adopted. This mission requires a stance of openness to whatever God gives them to bear—a submission of their will to the will of God. Based on this aspect of marriage, we look for the conversion marker in the couple of movement from inward focus on each other to outward mission to the world, starting with their home.

We will say much more about establishing a "domestic church" in chapter 8. For now, here are some reflection questions to help engaged couples discern their understanding of marriage as a ministry to the world and reflect on their task of making their homes holy:

- In what ways do I see our love for one another as a way we can help make the world a more loving and beautiful place?

- Am I ready to accept whatever circumstances may come to us and trust that God is with us through any challenges we might face?

- What is my own faith life like, and how do I see myself handing on that faith to my children?

  - What help do I need to strengthen my own faith?

  - What help do I need to be a good role model of faith for my children?

- What help do I need to be a good role model of faith for my spouse?

- What help do I need to be more comfortable in sharing my faith with my fiancé(e)?

- In what ways do I envision our home together as a place of prayer, spiritual nourishment, and service to the world?

What Are We Converting To?

For couples who do not have a living relationship with the risen Christ, they are converting to that relationship. For those who already have a relationship with Christ, they are continuing and deepening that relationship.

To have a relationship with Jesus means we have a commitment to dying. To follow Christ is to follow the way of Christ. And the way of Christ is toward the cross. And yes, the way of Christ also leads to the resurrection. But we have to be careful not to skip over the dying, especially when we are evangelizing those who are new to living a Christian life. We don't want to misrepresent. We don't want to make Christianity seem like it is always Easter morning. Or worse, merely a cultural convention that people "do" to please relatives or fit into society more easily. To follow Christ means to go to the cross.

The church has a term for this process: paschal mystery. To form people more closely into the image of Christ means training them to go deeper into the paschal mystery. Ask any group of average parish leaders to explain the paschal mystery, and most of them will tell you, almost in unison, that it's the passion, death, and resurrection of Jesus. And they'd be right. But what does that *mean*? How does that response touch the hearts of inquirers and draw them closer to this profound mystery of Christ?

You tell them a story.

Amy and Spenser

Amy and Spenser began bickering shortly after their marriage. Soon their bickering turned into full-scale conflict, with shouting, door slamming, and extended times of silent isolation. The things Amy once liked about Spenser now seemed to annoy her. His easygoing attitude now seemed to be just laziness and lack of diligence. And

Spenser, who was at first attracted to Amy's sharp intelligence and flair for organization, now saw her as "prosecutorial" when they argued and too much of a perfectionist about the way the house looked.

After seven years and two children, both were exhausted. A disagreement about how to discipline one of the children ignited their biggest fight yet. Afterward, Amy spent the night crying in their bedroom while Spenser tossed on the couch. Two days later, Amy told Spenser she wanted a divorce. Spenser didn't know what to say, but he didn't want to fight anymore. So he didn't say anything.

Amy put her organizational talent to work by researching divorce lawyers and Googling "divorce and children." She found an article on how to tell your children about your divorce and sat down with Spenser to discuss it with him. But he surprised her. He didn't try to avoid the topic or belittle it. Instead, he quietly started asking thoughtful questions and talking about his feelings.

"I feel defensive and small," he said, "when you keep asking me questions before I've finished what I'm trying to say. And I feel frustrated when you correct me and tell me what you think I really meant to say. How can I tell you what I'm thinking if I can't finish a sentence or if you won't accept what I'm saying?"

Amy wasn't sure she agreed with Spenser's premise, but she recognized that he was searching for a solution and not picking a fight. Once she saw that, she let down her guard a little and tried to find an answer that was both true and invited further conversation. "I was willing to try a little harder," she said later. "If he was going to work at solving this, so was I."

They put the divorce on hold for the time being and agreed to some clearer ground rules for arguing. They also agreed to seek out help to learn how to communicate better. Their fighting did not end that day, but their commitment to stop hurting started. Ten years later, they're still working at it. They have occasional flare-ups, but they get through them faster and with lots less drama. "Our marriage is a work in progress," said Spenser. "And our progress has been good. We're better than ever now. We're not perfect, but we're getting there."

Going to the Cross

For Spenser and Amy, something had to die before their marriage could live. They had to each die to themselves a little. They had to sacrifice their egos and their pride and their beliefs about who was right and who was wrong. This is a heroic thing to do. When we use the word "hero," we think of a firefighter rescuing a baby from a blazing house or a soldier taking a bullet to save his buddy. Most of us, though, will never be asked to make dramatic, newsworthy sacrifices. We'll never get a medal or a citation for *listening* to our spouse and trying to prove that he or she is right instead of wrong. But we are all asked to make *that* sacrifice—and dozens like it—every day. To be followers of Christ, we have to do what he did. We have to die to ourselves for the sake of the other. That is "paschal mystery."

What are the real stories of paschal mystery in your life? How can you share those stories with your engaged couples so they can recognize and enter more deeply into the paschal mystery in their lives?

This Won't Happen Overnight

Lasting change takes time. In the catechumenate process, those preparing for initiation spend at least a full liturgical year getting to know Christ and the church. The gradual nature of the process is key to the conversion of the catechumens. During this time, with the help of their sponsors and parish community, they discern the changes that are happening in their lives and how they are growing more and more into the image of Christ. Special prayers and rites throughout the process ritualize and strengthen the changes that are taking place.

With wedding couples, it's a bit different. Once an engaged couple comes to us, they're already pretty far along in their courtship. We've missed most of the gradual changes in their spiritual life and relationship because we're entering their story in the middle of it.

The six-month preparation period that many parishes require of engaged couples gives us some opportunities to witness their growth. For some couples who have been active in their faith, that's probably plenty of time for preparation. For many others, however, it seems like the preparation team is always playing catch-up, trying as best they can to get the couples up to speed spiritually. It does not seem to have that sense of gradualness that is key to conversion.

What if the parish could be more involved with potential marriage candidates at an earlier point in their relationships? What if we could accompany couples throughout the unfolding of their relationships and help mark significant moments?

Marriage preparation begins way before the moment a couple inquires about getting married in the church. You are doing marriage preparation whenever you grow your relationship with individual persons, couples, and families in your parish; whenever you speak about commitment, vocation, forgiveness, and sacrifice—and live them out in your own life.

Later in the book, we will give you some ideas on how to make your required time frame of proximate preparation a more gradual process. For our next step, however, let's take a look at the broad strokes of how to make the marriage preparation process a journey of deeper conversion to Christ.

3

How Do We Bring Couples to Deeper Conversion?

The Role of the Community of Faith

Another principle of the Rite of Christian Initiation of Adults is that conversion takes place within and because of the Body of Christ—the community of the faithful.

The RCIA gives specific ways the baptized can do this throughout the process. Here are some examples from paragraph 9:

- Show the spirit of Christian community.
- Welcome seekers into their homes.
- Talk with them.
- Invite them to the gatherings of the parish.
- Be present at the rites and prayers for them.
- Actively participate in Sunday liturgy.
- Be attentive to and name God's action in the seekers' lives.
- Be examples of Christian penance, faith, and love.
- Live authentically their baptismal vows.
- Help the newly initiated feel more at home in the parish.

If we take this principle of the catechumenate and translate it for our marriage preparation processes, how might this change what you currently do in your parish?

Most marriage preparation programs gather engaged couples together for a series of meetings, either with a couple alone or in a group of several other engaged couples. In these gatherings, they might meet the pastor or another person on the parish staff, a few other couples or persons on the marriage prep team, and maybe the liturgy and music director. They also might be invited to go on a retreat where they meet other couples perhaps from other parishes and other marriage preparation leaders in the community.

If the engaged couple are already well-connected to their parish community and know many people there, if they are participating regularly in the Sunday celebrations and other activities of the parish, if they are already strong in their faith life and share it readily with each other and those they meet, then this kind of discrete formation can be primarily what they need in order to live their new vocation within the community.

But let's be real. Many people who ask to be married in the church are not deeply connected to the community; many are missing from Sunday Eucharist; and many have not yet developed an adult faith that they feel comfortable sharing with others. For them, our focus needs to go beyond just marriage preparation. We want to draw them back into the life of the parish by reconnecting them (or introducing them for the first time) to the people who make up the parish community.

We're not talking here about getting them to know the community simply to have a feel-good experience or merely to recruit them into the parish so they become contributing members. The reason to connect them more deeply to the people of the parish is because we believe we are the Body of Christ. Our whole existence as church is to bring people closer to Christ who is present in his people. Ultimately, we want these wedding couples to feel at home with us and to know that they are essential to the life and mission of the church. So let's look at some ways to help these couples connect better to your parish.

Make Sunday Matter

Sunday Mass should be the primary gathering for those preparing for marriage. Without it, all your other preparation sessions lack a foundation because Sunday Mass is where they will most clearly see Christ at work in the world. Yet sometimes it's hard to convince couples that Sunday Mass is a priority, and many of them see little connection between what happens at Mass and what is happening in their own lives.

The solution to this is much bigger than the focus of this book. But there are definitely some things you can do right now to help make Sunday matter more to your engaged couples.

Resources for Helping People Realize the Value of the Lord's Day in Their Lives

Hudock, Barry. *The Eucharistic Prayer: A User's Guide*. Collegeville, MN: Liturgical Press, 2010.

Huebsch, Bill. *Whole Community Catechesis in Plain English*. New London, CT: Twenty-Third Publications, 2002.

Koester, Anne Y. *Sunday Mass: Our Role and Why It Matters*. Collegeville, MN: Liturgical Press, 2007.

Wagner, Nick. *Whole Community Liturgy: A Guide for Parish Leaders & Lay Ministers*. New London, CT: Twenty-Third Publications, 2005.

Wagner, Nick. *Why Go to Mass?* New London, CT: Twenty-Third Publications, 2010.

Think back to your first experience of Sunday Mass at your parish. What was it about that Sunday experience that made you come back again the following week? Gone are the days when people feel obligated to attend the church within the parish boundaries where they live. Many people will drive several miles each weekend to be able to go to a church that meets their particular spiritual needs.

What are those needs? The most-often cited needs that people are looking for in a church are good preaching, good music, and a friendly atmosphere. Other priorities are having a community where there are others like them, whether that is in age, ethnicity, language, spirituality, or social ideology; being in a church building that "looks like a church"; providing additional opportunities for gathering outside of Sunday Mass, such as social, spiritual, service-oriented, and formational groups.

Of all these priorities, which one do you think is the number-one factor in determining whether or not a first-timer to your parish comes back?

According to Chris Walker of EvangelismCoach.org, eight out of ten first-time visitors do not return to a parish because they felt that it was not friendly. Church Growth Institute, an organization that helps Christian churches use effective business practices to grow their congregations, interviewed these first-time visitors and asked them how they determined the friendliness of the community. The response of these visitors was simple and direct: "It was whether or not anyone talked to us."[1]

This is great news because it is a simple fix you can make next Sunday! You don't need a strategic plan to improve homilies; you don't need to get new musicians. You just need to be willing to talk to people you don't know.

So for your engaged couples who are not well-connected to the parish, make Sunday matter by making sure people in your parish talk to them. When engaged couples sense that parishioners are friendly and show some personal care for them, it's easier to get them to commit to making the Sunday liturgy gathering a priority. Do this by enlisting other couples and individuals who are not on staff or on the marriage prep team but who are "in the know" in terms of the parish community. That is, they're connected to other people in the parish and know something of the activities, culture, and history of the parish.

The job of these "ambassadors of welcome" is twofold. First, they engage with the couples by simply talking to them before or after Mass. These ambassadors should listen more than they talk. You or another person on the marriage prep team would initiate the introduction between these ambassadors and the couples. Then your ambassadors might ask some engaging but not intrusive questions to get to know them, for example, "What did you think of the Mass today?" or "Please tell me about yourselves."

Then the second part of the ambassadors' job is to introduce each engaged couple to another person or couple in the parish whom they think will connect well with the couple. The ambassadors might also tell the couple about a particular group or event of the parish that would interest them, and then introduce them to someone involved with that group or event.

Ambassadors of welcome are your networkers. Their primary goal is to connect your engaged couples more deeply but in a casual way with other people in your parish so that they will feel more comfortable and will begin to seek out their new acquaintances next time they are at your Sunday Mass.

Coffee Hour Caution

...advice for **greeting young adults** at church

✗ - *Avoid saying:*

"How old are you?"

Why: Is age so important? There's no good answer. Avoid this one altogether.

✓ - *Say instead:*

"What did you think of the service today?"

✗ - *Avoid saying:*

"Are you new here?"

Why: A young adult may have been attending for years, you just haven't met them. This implies you think they don't belong in the church.

✓ - *Say instead:*

"I don't think we've met, my name is..."

✗ - *Avoid saying:*

"When are you planning to have kids?"

Why: Having or not having kids is a private matter and not one people may want to discuss. This implies you only value young adults for their future children, not as a peer adult, here and now.

✓ - *Say instead:*

"What brought you here today?"

✗ - *Avoid saying:*

"What do you *do?*" or "What year are you in school?"

Why: For those who are un- or under-employed, work is a tricky question; assuming someone is a student implies you think they are of a certain age or life stage. Give them the chance to talk about whatever is meaningful, which might not be school or a job.

✓ - *Say instead:*

"So tell me about yourself..."

✗ - *Avoid saying:*

"We need more young people!"

Why: Like everyone else, young adults want to be seen for who they are, not as a token for their age.

✓ - *Say instead:*

"Great to meet you!"

✗ - *Avoid saying:*

"Have you met our other young adult?"

Why: Young adults enjoy friends of all ages. Welcome them into faith and fellowship.

✓ - *Say instead:*

"Can I introduce you to my friend?"

✓ DO: Introduce yourself • Make friends • Be interested • Reach out • Respect boundaries

 Office of Youth and Young Adult Ministries, Unitarian Universalist Association • uua.org/youngadults

More like "Happy Hour" and Less like Class

You can't force friendships upon people, but you can create opportunities for friendships to happen. A great way to help people, especially young people, feel like they belong to a community is by introducing them to people in the community in a setting that is more like "happy hour" and less like a classroom.

Think of ways you can incorporate more meal-sharing into your marriage prep sessions. In many TV sitcoms, there is always a scene where the friends in the show gather at a bar, coffee shop, restaurant, or living room to eat and drink together. Think of *Cheers, Friends, Seinfeld, Sex and the City, The Big Bang Theory*, and many others. The conversation and sharing are the focus; the food is just the setting. There's something about gathering to eat and drink together that helps people share themselves more openly. That's probably why the gospels have so many stories about Jesus at a meal or party and why Jesus chose a meal as the way his disciples should remember him.

Don't settle for just coffee and snacks before or after the meeting. Get people seated around a table, eating and drinking together.

When I (Diana) was in college, there was a program for students called "Dinner with 12 Strangers." The purpose of the program was to help make college a little warmer and friendlier. Alumni would sign up to host a meal for eleven other people made up of students, faculty, and other alumni. The host could cook the meal or buy the food and have it delivered or even get the meal catered. The food itself didn't matter. The point was to gather various strangers whose only commonality was that they were connected in some way to the college.

Before the meal, the host served hors d'oeuvres and let people mingle. At the beginning of the meal, the host asked an icebreaker question to get everyone sharing. These were risk-free questions that also revealed a little something of each participant's personality. For example, What has been your most memorable experience at our school?

Now, imagine inviting some of your newlyweds in your parish— those married five years or less—to host one of these kinds of dinners. (If having twelve guests feels too daunting, adjust it to something more manageable.) Invite two or three engaged couples and a few other couples from the parish. Some of these other parishioners might be those who are very active in a parish group. However, consider also inviting what we call "middle-pew" Catholics—those people who seem to always be at church but aren't always doing things at Mass or are already serving on multiple committees in your parish. You will find these people most often sitting in the middle of your church on Sundays. They're likely the ones who aren't already overcommitted to your parish but are often just waiting to be invited to do something, but not something too big or time-consuming.

At these meals, your goal is to connect your engaged couples with real people from the parish by having them talk about real things that matter. Other than your host couple and your engaged couples, your other guests do not need to be couples themselves. However, they do need to understand that the focus of the evening is on the engaged couples and their preparation.

How to Prepare a Meal Gathering for Engaged Couples

Before the meal, start with a simple meal blessing. Provide your hosts with some samples they can choose from and lead easily (see chapter 10 for ideas). Also provide them with some icebreaker questions to help people get to know each other a little bit. Next, have the hosts remind the participants of the purpose for the gathering, that is, to help and connect with the engaged couples during their preparation.

Have some discussion topics ready that would help couples talk about real issues but that also open the door for connecting those issues to faith. For example,

- Dealing with difficult family members
- Working through money issues
- Learning how to argue without hurting each other

Also allow the couples to present their own topics for discussion for use at that gathering or the next.

Because preparing for marriage involves many personal aspects, the hosts will want to share some guidelines with the participants so that all can feel comfortable sharing as much as they feel is appropriate for the group. Since a significant part of a good relationship is good communication, you might even consider sharing printed copies of these guidelines with the participants:

- Treat others as brothers and sisters in Christ, for that is who they are. As your brothers and sisters, commit to their well-being. Acknowledge that you might not be able to understand them fully, but you are committed to hearing their stories so you can understand them better.

- Commit to learning from one another. No one person has the complete truth about a topic, but each person brings his or her own gifts and perspectives to that topic.

- Listen more than you speak. When you listen, focus on the person speaking and not on what you will say as soon as that person is finished speaking.

Preparation Relies on Adult Learning and Requires an Adult Response

Another principle of the Rite of Christian Initiation of Adults is that the way of Christ is "a spiritual journey of adults" (RCIA, 5). Therefore, the conversion process uses the various ways adults learn, and it demands an adult commitment and understanding.

In church-speak, being an adult isn't determined by age. It's measured by one's ability to make specific choices based on one's understanding of the consequences. In other words, preparation is for those who can take responsibility for their own learning and their own choices. What does this mean for us who work with engaged couples?

1. Adults Learn Best When They Understand Why Something Matters

Don't give me just the facts. Tell me why this is important, and show me why it matters.

When we teach about Christian doctrines regarding marriage, we need to share the reasons why those doctrines matter to us. Married couples who have lived out these doctrines can be great examples, in word and deed, of why those teachings have mattered to them. What difference has following those teachings made in their own marriages? How have the things Catholics believe about marriage sustained them through difficult times? Then allow the engaged couples to imagine and discuss with each other why those teachings would be important for themselves in their particular situations.

This principle is important not only for teaching doctrine but also for giving reasons for liturgical regulations around marriage once you get to the ritual planning stage with the couples. Although not everyone might agree with the teachings or the regulations, the point is that you give them the "so what" reason for why these things are important for yourself so that they can assess, reflect on, and integrate them for themselves.

2. Adults Learn in Different Ways and Need the Freedom to Explore a Topic in a Variety of Ways

Let me learn it my way, and I'll care about it more.

In its wisdom, the RCIA honors this variety of learning by recognizing that formation happens not only in the classroom but also in prayer, when people form relationships with other Christians, and through personal witness and service to the world. This variety of "learning styles" gives adults many entryways into a particular teaching and deepens their curiosity and understanding of why that teaching would be important for them.

Adults learn in three basic styles:

1. Through what they see: Visual learners say, "Show me." They learn best from reading or writing about a topic, seeing images, diagrams, and models of the topic.

2. Through what they hear: Auditory learners say, "Tell me." Hearing a presentation and talking about it deepens their understanding about a topic.

3. Through what they do: Kinesthetic learners say, "Let me try." They want to practice the behaviors and skills involved in a topic. They thrive on role playing and group activities.

If your marriage preparation meetings use mostly one style of learning, see if you can try out some other ways of exploring the topic.

Ways to Explore a Topic

Ideas for visual learners:

- Watch a movie or read a story about the topic.
- Explore the church space, and look at the symbols and art.
- Study a diagram for effective communication.
- Share photos of other married couples.

Ideas for auditory learners:

- Invite married couples to share their stories.
- Interview each other and other people in the parish.
- Listen for a song at Mass about the topic.
- Take note of conversations that express patience, love, and commitment.

Ideas for kinesthetic learners:

- Role-play a scenario.
- Put together a symbol of the topic.
- Play a game.
- Take a walk as you have a conversation together.

As you incorporate a variety of activities into your process, also look at the wide range of activities your parish already does to help form people in faith. See chapter 4 for how to use your parish's weekly life as a training ground for marriage preparation.

3. Adults Learn from Experience

Give me something to do, and recognize what I've already done.
Although each person may have a preference for a particular learning style, the axiom is still true: "Tell me, and I will forget. Show me, and I will remember. But let me try, and I will understand." We learn by doing, and we deepen our learning by reflecting on what we did. We met a couple who had been married over fifty years. They held hands and looked at each other like they were still newlyweds. We

told them how much we admired their commitment. At that point, the husband said, with a twinkle in his eye, "We're still hoping it's going to work out."

No amount of reading, listening, or talking can teach us fully how to be married once the wedding is over. It's like learning how to drive a car. You don't really know how to drive until you actually get behind the wheel of a real car in real traffic with other real, fallible people . . . on a daily basis. And, you don't really know the consequences of what you've learned until you get into your first accident or have your first near miss.

We need to help couples practice the skills and attitudes of married life. They learn to forgive not simply by reading about forgiveness or talking about it or even understanding that they should forgive. They learn to forgive—and become forgiving people—by forgiving. They learn to sacrifice themselves totally to one another by sacrificing themselves in big and small ways to others each day.

As part of your process, encourage your couples to take the variety of learning experiences from their sessions and put them into immediate practice in their daily lives. Then provide opportunities at your sessions to have them reflect on their experience. What was most challenging? What was a blessing? What did the experience teach them about themselves, about their faith, about their commitment to one another? How was God present in their experience? What do they want to do differently the next time they have that same experience? In essence, what you are doing is mystagogy on their real-life experience. See chapters 6 and 8 for more information on the mystagogical process.

What this means for us, as leaders, is that we have to start from the experience of our couples and not be too hasty in beginning with our own agenda. Of course, we have certain topics we need to cover, paperwork to complete, and requirements to fulfill. But if we start with those things, we miss the opportunity to engage our couples more deeply by honoring their immediate needs, questions, concerns, and experience.

By listening first to their experience, we can pay attention to places where the topic we want to focus on in that session can directly connect. These connections strengthen their interest in the topic and give them a starting point from where they can build on their understanding.

When we set aside for a moment our prepared topics and put our couples' stories first, we are reminded that each person, each couple, is different and, therefore, each process for preparation must be different. When we keep that in mind, our sessions become less about getting married and more about becoming people of faith.

4. When the Time Is Right, Adults Will Learn

The teacher appears when the student is ready to learn.
This principle challenges our entire system of "how we have always done it." Marriage preparation is a requirement. Couples don't usually come voluntarily. They come because we tell them they have to.

What if we told them they didn't have to come? Well, that wouldn't solve the problem either. But what would happen if we could have "marriage preparation" even for those not trying to schedule a wedding in the next six months? What if your parish had two or three gatherings a year for couples who are dating who just want to learn how to deepen their love for each other in the context of their faith?

For example, imagine if you had a session for couples on how to argue. You could call it something like "Holy Fighting: How to Argue without Losing Your Love." Or a gathering on forgiveness called "How to Forgive When It's Hard to Forget." I bet you'll have lots of people ready to learn if you had a gathering called "What the Church Really Says about Sex."

These open sessions could supplement your formal marriage preparation sessions, and those formal required sessions will be more effective if your couples have opportunities to deepen their understanding throughout the year at sessions they *choose* to attend.

5. Adults Learn When the Process Is Positive and Encouraging

No one wants to feel stupid.
As adults, we're all supposed to know what we're doing, right? Well, imagine going back to school as an adult, or being in a group where you feel you're the only one who doesn't understand the topic but everyone else seems to be experts in it already. You can guess there would be a lot of apprehension.

Now imagine that the topic is your faith, religion, personal relationships, finances, childhood, and your sex life! How intimidating is that?! Now add on top of that the fact that this will happen at church with church people, some of whom are really holy, like priests, deacons, and nuns!

For some people (perhaps for many people), the church can be an intimidating place. And for those who have not been to church in a while or have never had any practice of faith, it can be daunting even just to walk through the doors, much less ask for help. For them, the church is a foreign place where they speak a language they don't understand.

You might have also encountered the flipside of this situation—those who treat going to the church like going to the shopping mall. It's no different than anywhere else, and making arrangements to get married there is just like ordering the flowers. It's just one more transaction in the wedding business.

For both these types of people, and for everyone in between, our response and responsibility to them is the same. Our job is to constantly and in every way possible show them the face of Christ from the very first moment they walk in the door or call us on the phone. From the young wide-eyed couple barely out of school to the couple with a few divorces between them, from the couple already with children to the overbearing mother of the bride, they are to be treated as though they were Christ for us. The doors through which we encounter Christ opens both ways.

Beyond showing basic respect and Christian care for all who come to us, here are other ways you can make the marriage preparation process more positive and encouraging:

- Be flexible with meeting times. Work around the couples' schedules.

- For your sessions, provide childcare for couples with children. Ask married couples from the parish and their older children or in-laws to assist with this.

- Avoid using church lingo that only "insiders" to Catholicism understand. When needed, explain terms; even basic words like "sanctuary," "tabernacle," or "vestibule" may be unfamiliar.

- Don't be condescending when someone doesn't know something very basic about the church or expresses a view that is counter to church teaching. Use active listening skills and nondefensive communication to build trust that may help the person to grow in understanding.

- Honor their privacy, and keep what is shared confidential.
- Keep them in your personal, daily prayer.

You're Never Going to Do This the Same Way Twice

When couples come to us, even if they have not been part of a religious tradition, God has already been at work in them. In some way, their appearance at your door is a response to God's action in their lives. Therefore, we need to honor the road that has brought them to that moment. Although there may be similarities among couples, the road for each couple, for each person, is different, and the path that we lead them on from there, necessarily, must be different for each couple and each person. Even though they already have the reception space booked years in advance and invitations already made, we cannot know how long their preparation for marriage will take. Nor will the same kinds of questions and exercises and retreats be as effective for every couple.

This is the final principle of the Rite of Christian Initiation of Adults, and one that is very important for our work with engaged couples. The way of Christ, the path to conversion, is different for every single person. We cannot offer a one-size-fits-all conversion process and expect anything meaningful to happen.

This is where our expertise and care come in. Our job is not to impose a preformatted process onto each couple—although that would be easiest to do and most efficient. If our goal is to help each couple respond to this vocation from God, we need to try to tailor our process for the specific personal, spiritual, and human needs of each individual.

Obviously, there has to be some knowable time frame for preparation. Yet if you have attended to the other catechumenal characteristics we have discussed here and have made the entire liturgical year and parish life the setting for ongoing preparation (see chapter 4), then the set period for immediate preparation can serve to solidify the progress already made.

No two couples are exactly the same because the Spirit is working in them in ways that are specific for them. Led by that same Spirit, we strive to shape for each of them a unique plan. In order to get a better sense of the specific movement of the Spirit in couples, the first few gatherings with them will require a lot less talking on our part and a lot more listening to their stories. Those stories will help to give us a roadmap for preparation tailored specifically for each couple's needs. In chapter 5, we'll give you a process for gathering their stories and using it to plan with them a course of preparation that will deepen their faith in Christ and their love for one another. For now, let's look at the tools you'll use in their formation.

4

The Four Indispensable Tools
of a Successful Marriage
Preparation Process

Previously, we explored what makes up the conversion journey toward Christian marriage. Here, we'll examine the four don't-leave-home-without-them tools you'll need to keep your couples on the right path. These four tools are going to sound familiar. Every parish uses them already. But we're not used to thinking of using all four of them for marriage preparation. However, if you can teach your couples how to use these tools during their preparation, they will serve them well in their marriage and will help them stay centered in their faith even when the road gets rocky or they lose sight of the path.

These are the tools you cannot do without:

1. Word
2. Community
3. Worship
4. Witness

Why Are These Four Tools So Powerful?

These four tools are the principle actions of the early church, distinguishing the first disciples as followers of Christ. Take a look at Acts 2:42-43, where we see that

They devoted themselves to
1. the teaching of the apostles

2. and to the communal life,

3. to the breaking of the bread and to the prayers.

Awe came upon everyone, and

4. many wonders and signs were done

through the apostles.

In the catechumenate, these four actions are the way we form new-comers into the Christian faith. By using these four tools already present in the Christian community, we give catechumens "suitable pastoral formation and guidance, aimed at training them in the Christian life" (RCIA, 75).

Because the catechumenate is our model and inspiration for all catechesis, we can use these same tools to assist in forming engaged couples for married life in Christ.

Word

When the church speaks about the "Word," it refers, of course, to the Scriptures. But if you read paragraph 75.1 of the RCIA closely, you'll see that this tool is more than just about reading the Bible.

The word of God is the fullness of God's revelation—which includes Scripture, church teaching, and the Logos, Jesus Christ.

If we confuse "Word" with "words," we can be misled to think that catechesis is primarily about giving catechumens words to read from Scripture or from the Catechism. While those might be important supplemental activities, the primary way we experience God's word is in the liturgy. The primary way Catholics "read" the Bible is liturgical. Revelation is more a communal act of listening carefully than it is a private reading. The goal is to strengthen our relationship *with* Jesus rather than just give us information *about* Jesus. And we interact with the Scripture and church teaching not only by studying it but also by living it in our daily lives.

This is why the RCIA says that a suitable catechesis is "gradual and complete in its coverage" (75.1). One cannot build a relationship with Jesus overnight. Like any relationship, it takes time and continues to grow even after many years. It's complete because this relationship needs to permeate the entirety of our lives, not just the times when we're happy or feeling holy or blessed, but also the times when we're angry and at our worst and lowest points of our lives. It can never be complete in the sense that we will know everything about Jesus and our faith, just as we will never know everything about our spouses. But with time and constancy in that relationship, we will know completely *who* Jesus is, *who* our spouses are, and what they mean to us in our lives.

How might a parish use the tool of Word to help engaged couples become that Word in their relationship with each other and with those they encounter?

The way in which catechumens are immersed in the fullness of God's revelation—in the Word—is through the celebration of the liturgical year. If the liturgical calendar is our system for using this tool of the word of God, then our use of that Word for marriage preparation should flow from the celebrations of the liturgical year. Sunday is the foundational weekly encounter with the Word. Perhaps your group gatherings with engaged couples might take place after the Sunday celebration and begin with a breaking open of the Word they heard proclaimed at Mass that day. This ensures not only that your faith sharing is connected to the church's encounter with Christ in the Word that day, but also that your couples know they are expected to be at Mass if they are to participate in the faith sharing on that Word during your session.

If you meet during the week, your marriage preparation sessions might incorporate a prayerful proclamation of Scripture from the assigned readings of that day. There are two calendars you can use for Scripture assignments. First, the weekday Lectionary gives readings for each weekday of the year that may be used at Masses or other liturgies of the Word on that day. Second, the Liturgy of the Hours may be another source for inspiring your celebrations of the Word at your sessions. Within the structure of Morning or Evening Prayer, you will find a collection of psalms and brief Scripture texts that rotate every four weeks and texts assigned for specific saints and days of the liturgical seasons.

Remember that the psalms—even if they are sung—are proclamations of the Word. People often will have an easier time remembering words of Scripture when they are set to music that they sing on a regular basis. Use your parish hymnal, and incorporate the psalm settings sung at Mass into your small-group prayer.

Whatever liturgical structure you use at your sessions, be sure to include some time for faith sharing on the Scriptures proclaimed. This might be a brief reflection on that Word given by one of the marriage preparation team members, some individual journaling on what they heard in the Word and its meaning for them, shared discussion about the Word between the partners, or a group discussion to break open the Word.

These individual and shared reflections on the Word then can become your springboard for going deeper into the teachings of the church, especially as it relates to the couples' married lives together. Imagine, for example, if last Sunday's readings were about Jesus feeding the huge crowd before him with only five fish and two loaves. The shared reflection among the group might lead to an extended discussion and catechesis on the church's teaching about stewardship or on any of the seven main themes of Catholic social teaching. You might then use that discussion to encourage the couples to discuss their hopes for their own households. What is their responsibility to those who are poor, and how might their lifestyle reflect their commitment to those who are hungry? What are some practical ways to talk about stewardship of their resources—of money, time, and gifts—so that their life together might be a blessing for each other and for those in need, in good times and in bad? What rituals do they want to practice together around meals? Do they want to consider some form of fasting as a spiritual discipline in preparation for their wedding?

Throughout their preparation, you might also take the various Scripture options from the wedding Mass Lectionary and use these in your gathering prayers. Start with the gospel reading options, and use the "Breaking Open the Gospel" exercise in the sidebar to help the couples break open the meaning of that reading for them. They might keep a journal (either one shared between them or private journals) with their reflections on each reading. Once they have gone through each gospel reading option, they can use their journal to select which gospel reading would be the most appropriate choice for their wedding liturgy. You can also do this exercise with the other readings from the wedding Lectionary.

Some Notes to Give to Your Couples about Readings for the Marriage Liturgy

- Only readings from the Bible may be chosen.

- There may be three readings. The first reading is from the Old Testament, except during the Easter season when it is from the book of Revelation.

- Note the days in the liturgical year when the ritual Mass for Marriage may not be used and those days when the full set of assigned readings for that liturgical day must be used, even in the Order of Celebrating Marriage without Mass.

- Although a list of recommended readings is given in the Order of Celebrating Marriage, on days when it is permitted, there is no prohibition to using other Scripture texts that may be meaningful for the couple. At least one reading that explicitly speaks about marriage must be chosen (see Order of Celebrating Marriage, 55; 56 also gives a listing of readings that particularly express the dignity of marriage).

Breaking Open the Gospel

This is a process couples can do together on their own or in small groups with other couples and team leaders during their marriage preparation sessions.

Prepare

1. Have Bibles or copies of the gospel reading ready for each person. If reading from Bibles, it's best that everyone uses the same translation to facilitate easier discussion, but having a variety of translations might also add to the depth of discussion.

2. Part of the exercise invites participants to underline words and phrases from the reading. If participants do not want to write in their Bibles, have paper and pens available for writing notes.

3. Provide some basic background material on the gospel reading. This can be found in many Lectionary commentaries, homily resources, or at the beginning of each book in the Bible.

4. Create a quiet and prayerful space for this activity. Include a place of honor for the Bible in the prayer space.

Gather

5. Silence phones and other electronics. Light a candle.

6. Pray for the Holy Spirit to fill your time together.

Proclaim

7. Have one person read the gospel passage aloud. All are invited to close their eyes and just listen to the reading without following along in their Bibles.

8. After the reading, allow for about twenty seconds of silence.

9. Have a second person read the same gospel passage aloud. This time, group members follow along from their own copies of the reading.

10. After the reading, invite members to underline words and phrases that strike them from the reading.

11. Together, they all share what struck them about the reading and why.

Reflect

12. Discuss what is going on in the world right now that needs to hear this gospel reading.

13. Discuss what is going on in your own life right now (at work, at home, in your family) that needs to hear this gospel reading.

14. Discuss what was going on in the life of the communities that the gospel reading was originally trying to address and any other exegetical or liturgical background for the readings. Use commentary resources to aid this discussion.

Discern

15. Based on these discussions, invite each couple to discern the "message" that God's word is trying to communicate specifically to them in this particular time in their relationship. There

are no wrong answers. (If this becomes the gospel reading for their wedding, the message they discerned becomes a key point in the homily.)

16. Each couple looks at the reading again and underlines a sentence or two that seem to summarize and communicate the message they discerned. (If this becomes the gospel reading for their wedding, these sentences will be the most important ones for the reader to proclaim.)

17. Each couple writes in a journal (either a shared journal or individual journals) the message discerned from the reading and the sentences from the gospel that summarized that message.

Give Thanks

18. Pray, giving thanks for the Word present in your midst.

Formation Flows from Relationship

As your couples begin to experience God's revelation through the Word, they will grow in their relationship with Christ. As with any relationship, the more deeply we fall in love with someone, the more we want to know about that person. That is the basic dynamic of formation of catechumens, and it can be the dynamic for your engaged couples.

Try to let go of thinking of marriage preparation as a series of topics you have to cover. Instead, think of ways to introduce the couples to Jesus and ways you can answer the questions that relationship will generate. When your catechesis flows from their experience of the risen Christ (primarily in the liturgy), then you begin to help them see the connections between

1. what they pray;
2. what they believe;
3. and how they live out their faith in their daily lives.

The Sunday homilies can also strengthen this threefold connection. If, as part of their preparation, your couples are regularly participating in your parish's Sunday Mass, your homilists can take part in the couples' sacramental preparation by preparing homilies with them in mind. Even if your homilists do not single out the presence of these engaged couples preparing for marriage, your assembly will certainly have other couples who are considering marriage, as well as those who are already married and those whose marriages are struggling. If we can weave their stories of commitment and doubt, ecstasy and anger, fullness and barrenness into the church's stories of faith, it will change couples. It will give them hope; it will deepen their faith; it will inspire them to live out their mission.

Remember, too, that our understanding of the word of God is also shaped by our nonverbal communication about that word. In the liturgies you celebrate, either with the parish or in your small-group sessions, what kind of book do you proclaim the Word from? Is it a dignified ritual book or Bible, or is it a photocopied page? Is the book you use for the proclamation of Scripture lovingly carried and kissed, enthroned on an ambo or prayer table? Or do you put it on the floor under a chair once the proclamation is finished? Our actions do indeed speak and teach.

If they do not already have one of their own, consider giving each couple a Bible for reading and praying with at home. Make the giving of the gift a ritual act. Perhaps a sponsoring couple from the parish, the parents of the couple, the priest or deacon who will witness the marriage, or another significant person in their life might be invited to provide a beautiful family Bible for the couple. In a simple ritual that takes place at a small-group session, proclaim the Word from that Bible and then solemnly present it to the couple. Conclude the ritual with a prayer over them, asking God to fill them with the Word so they might continue to proclaim that Word by their lives.

Encourage the couple to make this Bible a visible presence of Christ with them so that it doesn't become just another book on their shelf. Give them ideas on how to create a prayer space in their home where the Bible may be "enthroned" and used for daily prayer and reflection. Show them how to find the readings of the day in their Bible and online so they can pray along with the church wherever they go.

Community

The second tool that you already have in your parish and can use to prepare your couples for marriage is your parish itself. There are two ways to think of including your parish members in the marriage preparation process: directly and indirectly. Direct methods concentrate on inviting parishioners into the marriage preparation gatherings and processes. In chapter 6, we'll focus on a direct method that incorporates "sponsor couples" into your preparation process.

Another way you can directly involve parishioners is to create a "Wedding Welcoming Ministry" made up of parishioners who are available during those times when you have weddings scheduled in your parish. These would be hospitable persons who, perhaps, are older and have Saturday mornings free. Maybe it's someone who lost a spouse and wants to keep the spouse's memory in a special way by helping those who are getting married. Perhaps it's a newly married couple who have experienced an overwhelming and sincere welcome into your parish during their own engagement and want to give an hour of their time back to the church.

This Wedding Welcoming Ministry would arrive at the church about thirty to forty minutes before a wedding. They would assist in the parking lot to direct guests as they drive in and as they walk to the doors of the church. They'd be inside the church assisting with giving out programs, pointing out restrooms, and being a welcoming, friendly face at the outside and inside doors of the church. They might wear nametags or some other item that associates them with the parish. Once the wedding begins, they remain for about fifteen more minutes to assist any latecomers. Some might choose to stay until after the wedding to again greet guests as they leave the church and to help answer any questions that guests might have about the parish and its services. If some do stay for the wedding, they might be seated discreetly among the assembly to assist in the liturgical responses that might be unfamiliar for the wedding guests.

Direct methods like these are certainly effective in involving your parishioners. Indirect methods, however, tend to be more holistic and organic in their results because they change the way your parishioners look at what the parish does to minister to these marriage preparation couples and to married persons in general. These methods challenge you and your marriage preparation team to look at the current activities that already are happening in your parish—and the people involved in those activities—and to think of how those events and people might already be a way to help form couples for marriage. So instead of bringing parishioners into the marriage preparation process, you are drawing the couples deeper into the existing life of the parish and making that a significant part of formation for marriage.

Here's an exercise you can do to see how this indirect method could work.

The Parish as the Content of Formation

Get your parish's Sunday bulletin, and note all the activities that are happening this coming week—special liturgies, feast days, social gatherings, catechetical sessions, service events, concerts, committee meetings, and so forth.

Now ask yourself: What would an engaged couple learn about being a disciple, about being part of this community, or about being married by participating in this event? For example, at the feast of All Souls, they experience how the church remembers their ancestors in faith who have died and our understanding of the communion of saints. This can be the springboard for them to talk more about their families and who have influenced them in their faith and understanding of marriage. Or it could help them deepen their sense of unity with the Christian community. Perhaps it becomes a starting point for discussion on hope in the resurrection in the face of hardship, struggle, and even death. This hope can sustain them in their own relationship when there are challenges and moments of great loss.

Maybe this week, your parish is holding its annual festival. If your engaged couples volunteered to assist at one of the festival booths, who could they meet from the parish who might become a "sponsor couple" or who share common interests and might become friends who draw the couple deeper into the life of the parish? Who might give them some insight into commitment, both to another person and to the church?

Your parish is filled with so many activities beyond Sunday Mass and marriage preparation classes and so many people who are already active in their faith. Your parish and its daily work are the perfect training grounds for helping couples deepen their faith in Christ and their commitment to one another.

What difference might all this make in your marriage preparation process if you called forward more people from your parish to walk with these couples in these direct and indirect ways? Paragraph 75.2 in the RCIA gives us a glimpse of the effect. Let us reword it slightly for engaged couples:

> As they become [more] familiar with the Christian way of life and are helped by the example and support of sponsors, godparents, and the entire Christian community, the [engaged couples] learn
>
> > to turn more readily to God in prayer,
> > to bear witness to the faith,
> > in all things to keep their hopes set on Christ,
> > to follow supernatural inspiration in their deeds,
> > and to practice love of neighbor, even at the cost
> > of self-renunciation.

Summed up right there is the Christian way of life. You know people in your parish who excel in these practices. They will be your greatest assets in being a personal, human face of Christ for your couples, drawing them deeper into relationship with the church community. These parishioners need not be scholars in the teachings of the church nor moral theologians ready to defend its regulations. They only need to be prayerful, hopeful people, who love their Christian faith, believe that God is active in their lives, and try to love others even when it's hard. What better gift can you give to your couples than this?

Worship

The third tool in your parish toolbox is often overlooked because it is so familiar. It's your parish's prayer life. The heart of our Christian faith is our Sunday gathering. The fullest expression of the kingdom of God on earth is revealed when the church gathers on the Lord's Day to celebrate the Eucharist. In the Eucharist, the baptized exercise their priestly ministry by offering prayers for the world and giving their sacrifice of praise to the Father through Christ. By doing this in the Eucharist, not only are they nourished by the Body and Blood of Christ, but they too are transformed into Christ's body for the world. Having gathered on Sunday, they are sent into the world to put into action the prayers they had offered and to preach the Word and glorify God by their lives. In living their faith in this way, they continue Christ's mission of drawing all creation to himself that all might be one with the Father.

Sunday after Sunday, this is what happens . . . or at least it's supposed to happen. But Sunday has become a bit routine for too many parishes and their staff. It's simply one more thing the parish does among all the other things it has on its calendar.

But what if Sunday stopped being "one more thing" and instead became "The Thing We Do"? What if every ministry in your parish made Sunday its focus? What if they made Sunday the starting point of what they do throughout the week? The centrality of Sunday to the entire life of the church is what the Constitution on the Sacred Liturgy meant when it said that "the liturgy is the summit toward which the activity of the church is directed; it is also the source from which all its power flows. For the goal of apostolic endeavor is that all who are made children of God by faith and Baptism should come together to praise God in the midst of his church, to take part in the sacrifice and to eat the Lord's Supper" (10).

If this happened, it would absolutely change your parish. It would change your engaged couples' perspective on what it means to be part of your community. It might make them want to come back to your parish even after they're married.

But going from Sunday as routine to Sunday as The Thing is . . . well, a big thing. Here are some areas to tackle first if you're looking for a way to start.

Make Sunday the Hub

If you aren't already, consider holding your marriage preparation sessions on Sunday. Not Saturday afternoon, followed by Saturday evening Mass, but Sunday. We say that because usually the Masses on Sunday are more engaging and are better resourced than those on Saturday night. (But if the Saturday night Mass is your best Mass at your parish, then go for it!)

When you give your couples the schedule for meetings, make sure that your best Sunday Mass is listed as your start time for your session. Make sure that coffee and donuts, or whatever kind of parish social gathering you might have after Mass, is also part of your session.

Maybe for your first Sunday session, schedule your start time about half an hour before Mass begins so you or another person who knows the story of your parish can do a brief tour of the worship space. This tour isn't about showing your couples the church space as if they've never seen it before. They've surely checked out your space already to be sure it's suitable for their wedding. Instead, this tour is about revealing the things about the church they might have overlooked. On this tour, you'll use the church building to reveal who the people are that make up the church. If you connect the building with the stories of the people in your parish, then the place can come alive for your couples. It becomes more than just the church where they're getting married. It can start to become a place where they know the people and begin to make it their home for nourishing their Christian vocation in marriage.

A Story Tour of Your Church

Welcome your couples outside your church doors. If the weather is bad, begin your tour just inside the church doors. Go to each of the places below. At each place, share a bit of its symbolism and a story from your parish history. Then help them see a connection between this place and their marriage.

Use the stations below as templates to help you create and share stories about other significant symbols and places in your church.

You can do all the places in one tour or go through each place gradually and more thoroughly over several tours.

Doors

The Church's Story

Give some background on the church doors, such as:

> The doors of a church are symbols of Christ, who called himself a kind of door, a "sheep gate," when he spoke of himself as the Good Shepherd.

The church doors are where we first meet Christ as a community. They symbolize both an entryway into the church where Christ is present when the parish prays together and an entryway into the world where Christ is present when the parish lives and acts as his disciples in their daily lives.

Your Community's Story

Share the date when your church was dedicated. On that day, the bishop of your diocese officially opened and blessed your church by unlocking the doors in a special ritual. Tell something significant about the name of your church or the saint after whom it is named.

Their Story

Connect this place with their marriage using these or similar words:

At the church doors, we mark several significant life moments in a special way in our rituals. When an adult or a child wants to be baptized, we welcome him or her and the family first at the doors. When a Christian dies, we welcome his or her body again at the doors. And when a couple chooses to be married, we embrace them at the doors as they begin a new life together. All these life moments are transitions from an old life to a new one. The doors are a holy place marking that transition. Imagine the day of your wedding and walking through these doors. Know that the prayers of everyone who has walked through these same doors since they were first opened will accompany you as you move together into your new life.

Font

The Church's Story

Give some background on the church font, such as:

The font is where all Christians are born. The baptismal waters wash away our old life and give us a new life in Christ where we are no longer alone.

In the font, whether we were baptized in the Catholic Church or in another Christian denomination, we become brothers and sisters with one another in Christ, and because of that, we are committed to each other, no matter what, because Christ is committed to us always.

Your Community's Story

Tell a story about a baptism at that font that moved you.

Their Story

Connect this place with their marriage using these or similar words:

There are probably many reasons why you are asking to be married in a Catholic church. One of those reasons is maybe because the Christian faith has some kind of meaning and importance for you and your family. As you continue to prepare for your wedding, know that everyone who has been baptized in this font and in all the fonts in Christian churches around the world in history is praying for your happiness. For we believe that all the baptized make up the Body of Christ and the communion of saints. When one member of the Body rejoices, we all rejoice; when one member suffers, we all suffer. We pray for joy for you.

Ambo

The Church's Story

Give some background on the church ambo, such as:

The ambo is where the Scriptures from the Bible are proclaimed. It is also where a priest or deacon helps us to reflect on those Scriptures and find deeper meaning in them for our lives. Here, we also offer our prayers for the world and for one another.

The ambo is like a dining table, but what we feast on is God's word. The ambo is also like an altar because here we offer up to God the parts of our lives that need his love and intervention as well as the parts of our lives that bring us great joy for which we are grateful. Here, we know our prayers are answered because we read over and over again in the Bible how God has always been faithful and keeps his promises to his people.

Your Community's Story

Share a story about a particularly joyful or challenging time in your community. How was that experience brought to the community's prayer and how did the community show its trust and hope in God's faithfulness?

Their Story

Connect this place with their marriage using these or similar words:

> On your wedding day, you will hear several stories from the Bible. In each of those stories, God is promising to always love you. And in the prayers we will offer for you and your loved ones, we will promise to love you as well and help you strengthen your love for one another. As you continue to prepare for your wedding, listen for those promises that get spoken from this ambo every time we gather here to pray. Those promises are true because God is always faithful.

Altar

The Church's Story

Give some background on the church altar, such as:

> The altar is the heart of the church. This is where Catholics gather to give thanks to God, to remember what Jesus did, to pray for the Holy Spirit to make us one, and to share the Body and Blood of Christ in Communion.

> The altar is a special symbol of Christ because it is from the altar where we receive his Body and Blood. But it is also at the altar where we are most united as a family in Christ. This is why at the beginning of every Mass, the priest and other ministers kiss the altar or bow before it.

Your Community's Story

Tell a story about your pastor or other parish leaders or members who have gathered around that altar over the years. How has their presence in the community helped to reveal Christ's presence in that church?

Their Story

Connect this place with their marriage using these or similar words:

> In your home, your dining or kitchen table is a sacred place like this altar. It's where you will be nourished each day not just by food but also by your relationship with each other and with the family and friends you gather around that table. We treat this table here in the church with special reverence: we place a white cloth over it; we light candles around it and place only the finest vessels we can provide on it; and here we try to speak only words that will honor God. The next time you sit at your table at home, think of this altar. Then imagine ways that you can show to one another and to all who eat there that it is also a holy place where you are fed in body and spirit by your love for one another.

Pay Attention to Symbols

> [W]e might do well simply to recall that for most of our Catholic people, their religion is sustained, communicated and shared not primarily through doctrinal statements and creeds but rather through symbols, rituals, stories, metaphors and myths. . . . Surely the eucharistic texts are very important, but in many ways ordinary people's lives are touched above all when the new baby is born and baptized, when couples are joined in marriage, when close family members and friends have died and are laid to rest, when the sick and the elderly receive our Christian ministries. On those occasions it is the quality of warm hospitality and the power and beauty of the symbols and rituals that deeply touch people's lives. (Kevin Seasoltz, OSB, upon receipt of the 2009 McManus Award of the Federation of Diocesan Liturgical Commissions)

The language of ritual is made up of symbols. Symbols speak to the entire person and express multiple meanings that touch a person's mind and heart. Symbols, when used well and reflected on, open up a new way of seeing the world.

In liturgy, we need to pay attention to the symbols. As we see above, this is most important in those moments when a person's world changes.

Sunday Mass is our first priority. However, we also have to pay attention to the symbols we use for funerals, baptisms, anointings of the sick, and weddings. These are places where we celebrate life-changing moments. The liturgies that mark these moments are our chance—maybe our only chance—at making a difference in seekers' lives and drawing them one step closer to Christ.

Pope Francis spoke of the power of the liturgy, especially the sacraments, to teach and to strengthen faith:

> Faith, in fact, needs a setting in which it can be witnessed to and communicated, a means which is suitable and proportionate to what is communicated. For transmitting a purely doctrinal content, an idea might suffice, or perhaps a book, or the repetition of a spoken message. But what is communicated in the Church, what is handed down in her living Tradition, is the new light born of an encounter with the true God, a light which touches us at the core of our being and engages our minds, wills and emotions, opening us to relationships lived in communion. There is a special means for passing down this fullness, a means capable of engaging the entire person, body and spirit, interior life and relationships with others. It is the sacraments, celebrated in the Church's liturgy. The sacraments communicate an incarnate memory, linked to the times and places of our lives, linked to all our senses; in them the whole person is engaged as a member of a living subject and part of a network of communitarian relationships. (The Light of Faith, 40)

Use the symbols of the sacraments as doorways that help you and the church community enter into the lives of your couples and that help your couples enter deeper into the care of the church.

For example, use the wedding rings as a springboard for reflecting on the things we wear that communicate who we are and whose we are. Their rings tell others that they are vowed to each other. In a similar way, the cross Christians wear—better yet, the cross we place on our bodies every time we make the sign of the cross—communicates to others that we are promised to Christ. Invite couples to see their rings as a kind of sign of the cross they share: a sign of their deep, abiding love for each other, a love that calls them to lay down their lives for each other. In turn, invite your assemblies to reflect on the sign of the cross they make as a promise, like the promise symbolized by a wedding ring. Wearing that cross and marking themselves with it is a visible reminder of the promises they made to God and to one another, to love and honor God and their brothers and sisters in Christ all the days of their lives.

Make Liturgy Art

If symbols are the vocabulary of ritual, art is its grammar. In good ritual, there are four basic art forms that organize symbols into a cohesive liturgy: environment, movement, music, and words.

Environment

The art of environment involves all the physical things we see and touch and how we place ourselves in relationship to them. The place in which we gather and how we are arranged in it are symbolic. Because symbols teach, here are some things to pay attention to in our worship spaces:

- Treat the entire space as "holy." Don't place all your banners, flowers, candles only in the sanctuary. Find creative ways to highlight the area where the assembly sits, the aisles and entryways, and the doors to your church.

- Many churches have taken down the Communion rail, but almost as many have put up alternate barriers using a wall of poinsettias during Christmas, a fence of lilies at Easter, or a barricade of banners and candles surrounding the altar. Whatever you use to enhance the space should not create a visual or structural barrier either between the assembly and their participation or the ministers and their duties during the liturgy.

- Don't forget your parking lot, walkways, vestibule area, restrooms, and other gathering areas. Well-tended transition and gathering spaces also help your assembly prepare to pray well and leave your church feeling ready to do the work of faith in their daily lives.

- Remember that the minister of the sacrament of marriage is the couple, not the priest or deacon. Therefore, the couple should be seated in a similar way as we seat the priest or deacon in a liturgy. That is, they should be visible to the assembly and seated within or near the sanctuary so that it is clear they are assisting the ordained minister in leading the Order of Celebrating Marriage and participating fully as members of the assembly. The bride and groom would not have their backs to the assembly or be kneeling during the entire liturgy.

Encourage your couples to pay attention to the environment in their homes, and help them create sacred spaces that will serve as reminders of God's presence in their lives and their connection to the church community. A good starting place is the dinner table. Invite them to make at least one of their meals together each week at home a clearer reflection of the Eucharist by attending to the environment. Here are some ideas:

- Make a promise to keep the TV turned off and cell phones silenced and put away during the meal.

- Prepare the dinner table with your nicest table cloth and napkins, dishes and silverware. Bring out your best drinking glasses. It doesn't matter that there's no special occasion. Set the table in a formal kind of way, as if someone important was coming for dinner.

- Light candles, and put fresh flowers on the table or in the room.

- Dress nicely; it doesn't have to be fancy, just something that shows you are attending to not only how you prepare the table but also how you prepare yourselves.

- Have nice music playing in the background that enables conversation.

- Begin or end with a prayer of thanksgiving for the food (see chapter 10).

Movement

Symbols do not speak by themselves. How we use them and perform the gestures that surround them communicate meaning as well. Even those who have little religious formation can get the basic meaning of what is happening in the ritual simply by looking closely at the way we do the ritual and how we handle and use the symbols. It makes a difference in the hearts and minds of those witnessing the ritual when we take care and time in our gestures. Pay attention to your actions, gestures, movements, and postures throughout your Sunday and other sacramental liturgies. For example:

- Show the joy! We have the best message to communicate to the world as we share in the best gift ever given to humankind! Inform your face, and let others know you believe what you're saying and doing by how you look. Pay attention to this also during those times when you're "not on," that is, when you're not the focus and you, yourself, should be focused on another minister doing his or her role in the liturgy. Just like dance partners, each partner stays focused even while the other takes the spotlight.

- Walk with dignity and grace. A beautiful thing about Catholic processions is that they are wonderfully inefficient. They're never simply about getting from one place to the next. Rather, they ritualize the Christian's ongoing, lifelong journey toward God until we finally come to rest in him in the kingdom. Like a pilgrimage, the destination is not the only important part of the trip. The journey itself is formative. So take time with your processions. Make them look like processions—solemn but joyful, determined but not rushed. Don't always take the quickest, most efficient route.

- Practice custody of the hands. You've seen it done at the font, the beginning and end of Mass, at the gospel reading—making the sign of the cross looks a bit more like brushing away an annoying gnat than the profound symbol it is. Pay attention to your own ritual gestures and movements. Take time doing them, and make them big and intentional. Do the same when bowing or genuflecting and when you share the sign of peace with another.

Help your couples practice symbolic actions and gestures in their daily lives as a way to help them transform their entire lives into a reflection of God's abiding presence. Here are some ideas:

- All Christians begin their lives in water by being baptized with water and the invocation of the Trinity. Invite your couples to remember their baptism and give thanks for the gift of water and life whenever they shower or go for a swim or even wash the dishes.

- Lighting candles is a ritual action. Every time they light candles, ask them to give thanks for this first gift of God's creation and for their godparents, who first held the light of Christ for them. (See chapter 10 for a short prayer for lighting candles.)
- Teach them to bless one another, by showing them how to make the sign of the cross on one another or laying hands on their partner's head in prayer and blessing. Give them ideas for when they might bless one another in this way, for example, before one leaves for a trip, on a birthday or anniversary, when one receives bad news, in thanksgiving for good news. (See chapter 10 for ideas.)

Music

Sometimes we treat music as an add-on to the liturgy, something nice to do if we have time and the people to do it. But the liturgy itself is musical:

- The first thing to sing are the dialogues, such as, "The Lord be with you," "And with your spirit."
- Next, sing the acclamations and antiphons, such as the Holy and the psalms sung during the processions and between the readings.
- And don't forget the litanies, like the intercessions or *Kyrie*.
- Only last in order of preference are the hymns or songs we typically think of when we think of music at Mass.

Sung prayer, even a simple chant, does three things:

- It elevates the solemnity of the liturgy in a way that is accessible.
- It increases the participation of the assembly because communal singing naturally raises the volume level of a group.
- It strengthens the assembly's sense of unity because singing together requires people to breathe together.

As you are assessing your Sunday liturgical music, here are some things to keep in mind:

- There is no preferred style of music when it comes to Mass. There are principles that need to be followed to determine whether a piece of music is appropriate for Mass, but the primary aim for any decision in the liturgy is whether it enables the full, conscious, and active participation of the faithful. Determine what style of music and what songs help them best participate, and use those frequently. But also nourish and challenge them with other styles that come both from our rich history of music and from new composers.

- Singers who are amplified so loudly that they cannot hear the assembly singing become a distraction to the assembly and communicate to them that their participation in the song is not necessary. Instead, let the singers support and animate the assembly's singing. Remember that the assembly is the primary music minister in the Mass.

- In too many cases, we've conditioned our assemblies, both in religious and secular situations, to "leave the singing to the professionals." But time and again, music ministers have told us—and we've experienced it ourselves—that if you give an assembly a song they love and know, they will sing it strongly even without someone to prompt them. Furthermore, if you stop playing in the middle of the piece so that the assembly is singing *a cappella* (without accompaniment), they will sing louder! The key is to choose music they know and love and to let them know in words and actions that they are the primary music makers; the choir is only there to get them started and enhance the sound they already make.

Your couples might be thinking that the music for their wedding is more akin to a musical performance and the singers they hire are more like professionals who fill in particular moments with special music, like a movie soundtrack. But you can help them approach liturgical music in a different way and enhance their prayer life by giving them a different relationship to the music we sing together at Mass. Here are some ideas:

- Invite them to pay closer attention to the music sung at Sunday Mass. Which songs do they like? Which ones lift their hearts?

- Give them one of your parish hymnals to borrow. Ask them to read through the words of some of the songs. You might give them a few specific songs to look at, or invite them to remember the songs from the previous Sunday. Show them how to read the lyrics prayerfully in a kind of *lectio divina* using the words of the song. Ask them to do this each week, either together or individually, as a prayer discipline.

- Teach them a simple refrain or stanza of a song that praises God. Ask them to sing that refrain or stanza (or speak the words) as a prayer of thanksgiving before eating together.

Words

Ritual words are different than many of the kinds of words we use each day. Ritual words are symbolic in the sense that they have a deeper meaning than just the definition of each word. Ritual words are formational rather than informational; they shape a new reality that isn't seen just with the eyes. Ritual words are performative in that what you say and mean actually happens. Ritual words change things; they change people and their relationships.

For example, "Please pass me the water" is ordinary speech that means nothing more than what it says. But when you say, "I'm sorry," and "I forgive you," something more happens in that exchange of words. Words like these transform the relationships. What had been broken becomes healed.

We learn ritual words from our first significant relationships— those with our family—and the rituals we celebrate together at significant moments in our lives are filled with these kinds of words that give deeper meaning to the past, present, and future.

All the words we speak in liturgy are meant to be these kinds of ritual words, from the beginning of the Mass to the end. In the context of the liturgy, our speech takes on a different quality. There are more formal words that are prescribed by the ritual. But there are also less formal words but should be no less prepared and planned. Pay attention to these moments:

- Begin Mass with words of faith. Don't let "The Lord be with you," "And with your spirit" get diminished with add-ons like "Good morning," "Good morning, Father."

- If you want people to stand, don't say, "Please stand." Just raise your arms in a confident way. Use your eyes and your body to communicate instead of your mouth and the mic.

- Connecting with the assembly and putting them at ease are good things. But telling jokes is not the ritual way.

What are some ways you can help your engaged couples look at the ritual words they use in a different light? Here are some ideas:

- It's popular these days for couples to make up their own wedding vows. If this is something your couple wants to do, don't discourage them but invite them to use these at the rehearsal dinner or another appropriate gathering instead of at the wedding rite. In the liturgy, use the prayer of the church. The vows the church gives us in the Order of Celebrating Marriage symbolize the long line of husbands and wives who have made those same vows over the centuries and now stand with this couple as they take on the same responsibility.

- Encourage couples to memorize the vows the church gives them to say in the wedding rite. It is a more powerful statement for the bride and groom to memorize the words and say them without audible prompting by the minister. Also, in memorizing them, the couple is challenged to internalize those words and reflect on them gradually over time as they work to commit them to memory. Reassure the couple that you will have the words written down for them in large print on a piece of paper in the minister's binder in case they forget any part of the vows and need some prompting.

- Invite your couples to reflect daily on the words they say to each other. Do the words they say bring joy to their partner? Do they lift up and encourage? Do their words build up confidence and inspire hope in the other? Are their words authentic and true? Do they strive to say what they mean and do what they say? Perhaps invite your couples to use the "Prayer for Good Speech" (see chapter 10) as a daily prayer each morning for a period of time during their engagement.

Three Little Words

"And I want to repeat these three words: please, thank you, sorry. Three essential words! We say please so as not to be forceful in family life: 'May I please do this? Would you be happy if I did this?' We do this with a language that seeks agreement. We say thank you, thank you for love! But be honest with me, how many times do you say thank you to your wife, and you to your husband? How many days go by without uttering this word, thanks! And the last word: sorry. We all make mistakes and on occasion someone gets offended in the marriage, in the family, and sometimes—I say—plates are smashed, harsh words are spoken but please listen to my advice: don't ever let the sun set without reconciling. Peace is made each day in the family: 'Please forgive me,' and then you start over. Please, thank you, sorry! Shall we say them together? [They reply 'yes.'] Please, thank you, and sorry. Let us say these words in our families! To forgive one another each day!" (Address of Pope Francis to the Participants in the Pilgrimage of Families during the Year of Faith, Saint Peter's Square, October 26, 2013)

Witness

The last tool in your parish toolbox is witness. In a way, this is the most important tool of the four. Without it, the other three tools would have limited effect. If all your parish members, including your couples, honed their skills at being disciples by using only the tools of Word, community, and worship, they would still be incomplete in their work as disciples. The entire point of following Jesus is to be witnesses in the world by our actions and words of the saving power of Christ to transform death into life. Praying, studying the Word and our faith, and living in love with other disciples are important facets of Christianity. But these can become inward-looking actions that keep disciples to themselves if they did not also become witnesses. Disciples are those who do all these things in order to be equipped to go out to those outside the community of disciples and share how their life has been transformed by this way of life.

Before his ascension, Jesus gave one last command to his disciples that summarized the entire way of life for those who would follow him: "Go, therefore, and make disciples of all nations, baptizing them in the name of the Father, and of the Son, and of the holy Spirit, teaching them to observe all that I have commanded you" (Matt 28:19-20).

According to Jesus' command, his followers are to

- go;
- make disciples;
- baptize them;
- teach them.

However, Father Mike Fones, a Dominican priest who speaks on evangelization, noticed something unusual in the way we have tried to follow Jesus' command. He saw that in our formation processes, especially those for initiation, we have gotten the steps of Jesus' command reversed. We teach them, baptize them, and then they leave without having ever learned how to be disciples. They disappear until they need the next sacrament. We can't really fault them if we started with the wrong task (teach them) and the wrong goal (baptize them, confirm them, marry them).

We have to start in the right place (go) with the right goal (make disciples), and we have to start with ourselves. Are we "going" and "making disciples"? Are we living an apostolic life?

The RCIA gives us a one-sentence summary of what an apostolic life looks like when it tells us what the catechumens should be learning in order to be true disciples of Christ: "Since the Church's life is apostolic, catechumens should also learn how to work actively with others to spread the Gospel and build up the Church by the witness of their lives and by professing their faith" (RCIA, 75.4).

Therefore, you, your parish leaders, and all the baptized in your parish should be

- working with others;
- to spread the Gospel;
- and build up the church;
- by what people who have not heard the Gospel see you do and hear you say.

The first step in making disciples is simply to go. Pope Francis spoke about this in his interview with *La Civiltà Cattolica* in August 2013:

> I see clearly . . . that the thing the church needs most today is
> the ability to heal wounds and to warm the hearts of the faithful
> . . . You have to heal [their] wounds. Then we can talk about
> everything else. . . . The most important thing is the first proc-
> lamation: Jesus Christ has saved you. And the ministers of the
> church must be ministers of mercy above all. . . . Proclamation
> in a missionary style focuses on the essentials, on the necessary
> things: this is also what fascinates and attracts more, what makes
> the heart burn, as it did for the disciples at Emmaus. . . .
>
> Instead of being just a church that welcomes and receives by
> keeping the doors open, let us try also to be a church that finds
> new roads, that is able to step outside itself and go to those who
> do not attend Mass, to those who have quit or are indifferent.[1]

How, then, can we help one another, as well as our engaged couples,
have the audacity and courage to go outside of their usual circles to
heal wounds and give that first proclamation? Here are some ideas
for you and your parish leaders:

- Make hospitality everyone's responsibility. Don't just leave it
  up to a small team of people.
- Make hospitality less about coffee and more about conversa-
  tions. Food is good, but the people are the most important part
  of hospitality.
- Give parish leaders a witness challenge:
  - Meet at least two new people at Mass every Sunday.
  - Talk about your personal relationship with Jesus to at least
    one person each week.
  - Talk positively about the parish, something you are doing
    at church, some Christian practice you are exercising, or
    something about the pope or the worldwide church to
    someone you don't usually talk to about those things.
  - Take one risk each week to heal another person's wounds.
  - Review the parish's budget and the stewardship of our own
    resources. Is sacrifice and service to those in need integral
    to the preparation of the budget?

Here are some ideas to do with your engaged couples:

- Ask couples to participate in one of the parish's service ministries. Provide opportunities for reflection with other couples on their experiences afterward.

- Ask couples to reflect on why celebrating their wedding in the Christian community is important. Note any deepening in their understanding of their vocation. Ask them to share their responses with the wider parish community, either as a written reflection in the bulletin or a "witness talk" at Sunday Mass or another parish gathering.

- Invite your couples to take on the same witness challenge given above to the parish leaders.

- Ask your couples to discern a few creative ways they could use their wedding preparation and celebration as opportunities to heal wounds, for example:

  - Reconcile with a family member who has been estranged from their lives.

  - Make a sacrifice in their plans, and use the extra money, resource, or time to help others in need. For example, purchase fewer flowers or different, less expensive flowers, and donate the money saved to a local charity. Or spend part of their honeymoon learning about the economic struggles of those who are poor in the place they are visiting, and make a commitment to help in some way.

  - Invite guests to get involved in a charitable event or organization that is important to the couple.

  - During the wedding liturgy, include intercessions for those in need.

  - If they are celebrating their wedding within a Mass, consider inviting the couple to take up a collection (of money or goods) for a particular cause that alleviates the suffering of those in need. As the collection basket is brought forward, the couple also places their offering into the basket.

  - In their discussion about financial practices, encourage them to reflect on how developing a household budget is a moral act.

As your couples engage in this kind of witnessing, help them develop a lifestyle of witness so that the actions they practice during their engagement continue on throughout their marriage and shape their understanding of their mission to the world as married couples.

Setting Hearts on Fire

Our couples already come to us with hearts on fire with love for each other and a desire to celebrate that love in the rituals of the church. Your call as ministers responsible for their vocational preparation is to give them all the tools they will need to keep that fire burning. The four tools of Word, community, worship, and witness will help them open their hearts even more to be kindled by the fire of the true Christian spirit, which we learn through our full, conscious, and active participation in the liturgy and life of the Christian community.

If you help your couples make use of these tools during their engagement, their wedding liturgy will be more than just a ceremony. It will be where they will gather with the community to hear the Word and sacrifice themselves with Christ to bring healing to the world. These are the essentials, the "necessary things," as Pope Francis said, that help us make that first proclamation in our daily lives of the saving power of Jesus.

5

Inquiry:
How to Start Off on the Right Foot

The Rite of Christian Initiation of Adults gives us a very clear roadmap for the journey of preparation for baptism. The road-map sets up goals and markers that lead an unbaptized person deeper into a life of conversion to Christ. We can use a similar roadmap with our engaged couples to lead them deeper into a life of holiness as married persons with their own order and place among the people of God (see Order of Celebrating Marriage, 8). To give us a sense of what this marriage prep roadmap looks like, let's take a brief look at the RCIA roadmap.

Four Stages of the RCIA

The stages of the RCIA are designed for unbaptized adults and children who have reached the age of reason. Those who are already baptized but have received no further catechetical formation since their baptism might go through a similar process that is found in the second part of the ritual text for the RCIA, but we always honor their status as baptized members and therefore members of the faithful, distinct from those who are unbaptized. (The RCIA does not address those who are baptized and have had some form of catechesis already during their life. These persons go through a period of sacramental preparation not found in the RCIA. This preparation also focuses on continued conversion to Christ, but the time frame, context, and process build on their baptismal status and level of formation.)

The four stages of the RCIA are:

1. *Evangelization and Precatechumenate:* a period of inquiry between the Christian and those seeking a deeper relationship with Christ

2. *Catechumenate:* a period of training in the Christian way of life through reflection and study of the Word, engagement with the community, participation in the liturgy and daily prayer, and witness by word and deed of the faith they have already received

3. *Purification and Enlightenment:* a short period of intense prayer, fasting, and works of charity supported by the community's ritual prayer that helps the catechumens remove any obstacles to their faith and strengthens them in their perseverance to follow Christ

4. *Postbaptismal Catechesis or Mystagogy:* a period that leads to an ongoing lifestyle of recognizing God's saving actions in one's life and lifelong deepening of faith and understanding of discipleship

The Roadmap for the Marriage Preparation Journey

If we use this template to develop a roadmap for marriage preparation, it could look like this:

1. *Evangelization and Inquiry:* a period of inquiry between the Christian community and those seeking to be married within the Christian community

2. *Mentoring in Married Life:* a period of training in the Christian married way of life through reflection and study of the Word, engagement with married couples and others in the community, participation in the community's liturgy and the domestic church's prayer life, and witness by word and deed of the faith they continue to develop

3. *Ritual Preparation:* a short period of spiritual preparation that includes intense prayer, fasting, and works of charity supported by the community's prayer that helps the couple remove any obstacles to their commitment and strengthens

them in their vocation; also includes immediate preparation for the rite with family, friends, and community members

4. *Postsacramental Care:* a period that leads to an ongoing life-style of recognizing God's saving actions in one's married life and lifelong deepening of faith together and understanding of one's vocation

In this chapter, we'll take a look at the first stage in the RCIA and explore how that serves as a pattern for the first stage of marriage preparation.

Evangelization and Precatechumenate in the RCIA

In the first stage of the RCIA, there are three movements. The first is the continual movement of the church, that is, all the baptized. There is no beginning or end to this stage. We are always in this stage because we are always evangelizing. By our daily words and general actions, we faithfully and constantly proclaim the living God and Jesus Christ (see RCIA, 36). Having been mandated to glorify the Lord by our lives, we are specifically on the lookout for those in need, those who are physically, emotionally, or spiritually wounded. To them, we make a first proclamation that Jesus saves because Jesus had saved us. We proclaim the living God by healing the wounds of those we encounter.

Mercy above All

"The church sometimes has locked itself up in small things, in small-minded rules. The most important thing is the first procla-mation: Jesus Christ has saved you. And the ministers of the church must be ministers of mercy above all" (Antonio Spadaro, SJ, "A Big Heart Open to God: The exclusive interview with Pope Francis," *America*, September 30, 2013, http://www.americamagazine.org /pope-interview).

The second movement is that of those who are unbaptized who, in their ordinary encounter with a Christian, witness something a Christian does or says that sparks a response, a question, or a longing in themselves. That spark leads them to ask the Christian why they do what they do, what makes them live that way, and how they can have what they have.

Once that deeper question has been asked, the third movement occurs in which the Christian is compelled by faith to say, "Come and see." This third movement of this stage establishes a relationship, albeit initial, between the Christian community and an inquirer. This part of the precatechumenate is a time for these inquirers longing for that "something more" that Christians have to be introduced to the Christian community and the Gospel values by which they live.

In this third movement of relationship-building, the parish leaders also discern with inquirers their specific needs and longings and work with them to map out a process for helping inquirers meet those needs in Christ. Throughout this initial relationship with the inquirers, parish leaders are regularly watching for signs of spiritual growth and a deepening desire and commitment to live the Christian way of life. The parish community assists the inquirers in developing this initial growth in faith by giving them an explanation for why they themselves believe in Christ. The inquirers also meet other Christians in the community to help strengthen their desire to leave their old way of life and begin this new life in Christ. Throughout this stage, parish leaders and other community members assist the inquirers in discerning their own reasons for entering the Christian way of life and aligning them to Christ's mission. As it becomes clear that the inquirers are becoming more ready to take the first public step on their journey to baptism, the parish leaders discern appropriate companions (sponsors) from the parish community who will accompany the inquirers during the next stage of the preparation process.

Evangelization and Inquiry in Marriage Preparation

Let's take these three movements of the evangelization and precatechumenate period of the RCIA and translate them for a marriage preparation process.

If the baptized are constantly evangelizing, showing forth the living Christ in everything they say and do individually and as a community, what does it look like in a parish that continually fosters a sense of committed relationship among its disciples?

Now, you've seen all the wedding shows and you know that the wedding business is big bucks. And in order to have "the wedding of their dreams," major plans had already been made, sometimes years before: Save the Date cards were mailed so out-of-town guests could save up for travel expenses; banquet rooms were reserved with substantial down payments. By six months before a wedding date, there's almost no turning back for a couple and their families, who have already invested what may well amount to a year's salary for some people. If our preparation and discernment process began only at six months before, how can there be any real spiritual preparation and discernment for this couple? There's simply too much pressure to "go ahead" with the wedding because too much money has already been spent on it—not to mention the overall pressure and expectations coming from family and friends and the perceived embarrassment of calling the wedding off.

We suggested earlier that we begin "marriage preparation" much earlier in the process—even at the casual dating stage. Then we might be able to help couples notice how God has always been a part of their lives and now can be a part of their relationships. We could give them some tools and skills to use to express their faith with each other more readily, to forgive and ask for forgiveness more often, and to make their courtship a reflection of God's love more clearly. We could celebrate with them through prayers and blessings as they move from one level of commitment to the next.

Now imagine going even further back, accompanying them before they had even met each other. If marriage is a vocation, then the seeds of that vocation are planted in childhood. How do we help children and teens learn to form loving relationships? How do we support their parents to help them be the best examples of married life they can be for their children? In our parish and school staffs and organizations, how do we encourage respect for one another and model work styles that treat women and men as equals?

The Role of the Family and the Parish in Formation of Young People for Marriage

"So that the 'I do' of the spouses may be a free and responsible act and so that the marriage covenant may have solid and lasting human and Christian foundations, preparation for marriage is of prime importance.

The example and teaching given by parents and families remain the special form of this preparation. The role of pastors and of the Christian community as the 'family of God' is indispensable for the transmission of the human and Christian values of marriage and family, and much more so in our era when many young people experience broken homes which no longer sufficiently assure this initiation:

> It is imperative to give suitable and timely instruction to young people, above all in the heart of their own families, about the dignity of married love, its role and its exercise, so that, having learned the value of chastity, they will be able at a suitable age to engage in honorable courtship and enter upon a marriage of their own [Pastoral Constitution on the Church in the Modern World, 49]." (*Catechism of the Catholic Church*,[1] 1632)

Over the years, if your parish and parishioners can "evangelize" about the joy of unconditional love that calls us to sacrifice for one another, then, by the time a couple comes to us with their plans to be married, they already have a solid foundation for that vocation by the "formation" they have already received.

We can see you shaking your head and thinking, "This never happens!" You're lucky if the couple coming to you have even been to church since their First Communion or confirmation. A lot of times, you're doing not just marriage preparation but basic religious formation as well.

Don't give up on this process. Just as any conversion process takes time, so will changing the culture of modern Christian life today. This is exactly why we need to rethink our marriage preparation process so that "preparation" for marriage doesn't begin only when a couple contacts the parish to reserve their date, or takes place only at church in a meeting. Rather, let's see how we can show our care and concern for all those in relationships, especially our young people, Sunday after Sunday, year after year, in our daily words and actions, before they even begin to consider marriage. If this happens, we might begin to change our own relationship with our parishioners and what we do as a parish so that fewer people leave that relationship with the church. If we can do this, then the church doesn't just become the place where the wedding happens but the community where people have learned to love one another and to grow in holiness by that love.

Here are some specific ideas on how to make your parish a place where marriage is honored and unconditional love for one another is a hallmark of the disciple of Christ.

Mark Significant Relationship Moments

List as many significant moments in a couple's life that you can think of, from the first date to old age together. Which moments might be appropriately acknowledged in a parish celebration, for example, wedding anniversaries, engagements, preparation for birth? Which moments can be occasions for the family to pray together in the home, for example, first announcement of engagement, baby showers, heartbreak? And what are times when couples or individuals need special prayers or support, for example, miscarriage, breakup, loneliness, financial difficulty, severe illness or death of a spouse or loved one?

Now, brainstorm ways your parish community or pastoral staff can be present for these moments, directly or indirectly. Look at the liturgical year, Lectionary, and parish calendar, and note particular days when your parish can bless or pray for those going through a significant event or when the homily might draw upon a common experience in a couple's life. Provide written prayers and blessings that individuals and families can use at home to mark more private moments.

Some Significant Relationship Moments

- First date
- First kiss
- Leaving home
- Parents' divorce
- Parents' remarriage
- After a fight

- Meeting the parents
- Buying rings
- Engagement announcement
- Choosing your wedding party
- Getting a wedding license
- Finding out you're pregnant
- Moving into your first home
- Losing a job
- Getting hired
- Miscarriage
- Anniversaries in the first five years
- Death of parents and grandparents
- Death of a child
- Infertility
- Choosing a child's name
- Child's first words
- Child's first steps
- Child's first heartbreak
- Financial worries
- Discovering significant illness

Highlight Marriage as a Vocation

When most people think of vocations, they think immediately of ordained or religious life. However, since Vatican II, the church has taught that married life is itself a vocation that is "held in high esteem" (Pastoral Constitution on the Church in the Modern World, 49). In particular, it is a vocation of evangelization that is "accomplished in the ordinary circumstances of the world" in which husbands and wives are "witnesses of their faith and love of Christ to each other and to their children" (Dogmatic Constitution on the Church, 35).

Marriage as a Vocation in the Church

"The unity of marriage, confirmed by our Lord, is clearly apparent in the equal personal dignity which is accorded to [husband] and wife in mutual and unreserved affection. Outstanding virtue is required for the constant fulfillment of the duties of this christian calling. Married couples, therefore, strengthened by grace for leading a holy life, will perseveringly practice and will pray for a love that is firm, generous, and ready for sacrifice" (Pastoral Constitution on the Church in the Modern World, 49).

"Widowhood, accepted courageously as a continuation of the calling to marriage, will be honored by all" (ibid., 48).

"Let married people themselves, who are created in the image of the living God and constituted in an authentic personal dignity, be united together in equal affection, agreement of mind and mutual holiness. Thus, in the footsteps of Christ, the principle of life, they will bear witness by their faithful love in the joys and sacrifices of their calling, to that mystery of love which the Lord revealed to the world by his death and resurrection" (ibid., 52).

"According to their own vocation, those who live in the marital state are bound by a special duty to work through marriage and the family to build up the people of God" (Code of Canon Law, Latin-English Edition, New English Translation [Washington, DC: Canon Law Society of America, 1999], c. 226 §1).

Whenever your parish speaks of vocations to the religious life and holy orders, include marriage as one of the vocations in which Christians live out their call to holiness. If you have posters showing your diocese's seminarians or others preparing for religious life, consider adding alongside photos of your parish's engaged couples preparing for marriage, encouraging your parishioners to pray for both groups.

As you continue to lift up marriage as a holy "order," you can begin to plant the seeds of vocation to all the orders of the church in your young people and show that all the orders are necessary, sacred, and holy.

Marriage as an Order in the Church

"The word *order* in Roman antiquity designated an established civil body, especially a governing body. *Ordinatio* means incorporation into an *ordo*. In the Church there are established bodies which Tradition, not without a basis in Sacred Scripture, has since ancient times called *taxeis* (Greek) or *ordines*. And so the liturgy speaks of the *ordo episcoporum*, the *ordo presbyterorum*, the *ordo diaconorum*. Other groups also receive this name of ordo: catechumens, virgins, spouses, widows . . ." (*Catechism of the Catholic Church*, 1537).

"This is the reason why the Church normally requires that the faithful contract marriage according to the ecclesiastical form. Several reasons converge to explain this requirement:

- Sacramental marriage is a liturgical act. It is therefore appropriate that it should be celebrated in the public liturgy of the Church;

- Marriage introduces one into an ecclesial *order*, and creates rights and duties in the Church between the spouses and towards their children;

- Since marriage is a state of life in the Church, certainty about it is necessary (hence the obligation to have witnesses);

- The public character of the consent protects the 'I do' once given and helps the spouses remain faithful to it" (*Catechism of the Catholic Church*, 1631).

How Long Does It Take to Prepare for a Wedding?

I (Diana) used to work at a college campus ministry that had a gorgeous chapel on campus. If you wanted what some might call a traditional-looking wedding for your photos, this was the place: a long aisle, stately pipe organ, intricate altar area to serve as a beautiful backdrop for your wedding photos, lush garden outside. Part of my job was to schedule the events that took place at the chapel, including the weddings. Competition for one of the coveted wedding time slots was so fierce that the college instituted a strict reservation policy. To reserve the chapel for a particular date, one had to call the chapel reservation hotline exactly one year prior to the desired date—at 12:01 a.m.! Every morning, I'd check the voice messages on the hotline, and sure enough, there were a string of voice mails all coming in within the first five minutes after midnight. Sometimes, the message wasn't from the bride- or groom-to-be, but from a mother or a sibling or a friend. I imagined that some couples enlisted a whole gaggle of phone-callers to call on their behalf in the middle of the night to ensure that they would get the desired wedding date booked.

It seems there needs to be some middle ground between the 12:01 a.m. reservation process and the minimal no-turning-back six-month time frame.

If your parish has been doing ongoing "evangelizing" about the vocation of marriage, then you have the groundwork that will allow couples to enter into a true discernment and preparation process that relieves them of the pressure of meeting schedules and spending money they may never get back. In a parish that uses the catechumenate process as a model for marriage preparation, that ongoing evangelization leads to a preliminary stage of remote preparation that comes before the standard six-month time frame of immediate preparation.

This stage may be seen as a kind of "inquiry" period when the couple is discerning the possibility of marriage with each other and asking whether or not that is indeed the call for both of them. In other words, this period has them discussing "should we get married" and not "where and when can we get married."

A Discernment Gathering

During the year, couples are always contemplating these kinds of questions. So this stage really has no formal beginning or end. Therefore to help couples engage in these kinds of questions when they come up as they progress in their own relationships, your parish might consider hosting four or five gatherings during the year. These gatherings would follow a similar goal as other vocational gatherings for those discerning a call to religious life, namely, to explore what it means to live this Christian vocation, practical help for those wanting to know how to discern if this is the right decision for them at this time in their lives, and some information on the church's discernment and formation process for those entering into this vocation. You might call these gatherings "I Do or I Don't: Discovering If You're Called to Be Married" or "How to Listen to Your Heart before You Propose." These titles make it clear that this isn't an information session on the wedding preparation process but more about vocational discernment. Couples might attend together or separately. A similar gathering might be prepared for parents of young adults to help them learn how to help their children discern this major step in their life. The format should be casual and comfortable. Here's one possible 90-minute outline for the gathering:

- 10 minutes: Gather, introduction of facilitators, brief prayer (possibly based on Psalm 139)
- 5 minutes: Overview of gathering
- 10 minutes: Interactive presentation on what is Christian discernment

  - How do I follow my heart?
  - What do I need to let go of?
  - Is this God's call to me or me setting my own direction?

- 15 minutes: Small- or large-group discussion on current life circumstances; what are some things each person is seeking to discern in his or her life?
- 5 minutes: Break
- 15 minutes: Interactive presentation on the Christian vocation of marriage
- 15 minutes: Individual or partnered exercise (e.g., journaling, discussion questions, survey) exploring:

  - Where have I been in my life of faith, family, career, level of joy?
  - Where am I now in my life of faith, family, career, level of joy?
  - Where do I want to go in my life of faith, family, career, level of joy?

- 15 minutes: Large-group wrap-up

  - Presentation of resources for continued discernment

- Next steps for discerning marriage and beginning formal preparation for marriage
- Q and A
- Closing prayer

Imagine if a couple had participated in one of these kinds of gatherings a year to a year and a half before their desired wedding date. With this kind of spiritual formation, the couple have a better foundation on which to build their vocation to married life.

When Couples Inquire about Getting Married in Your Parish

When couples call your parish office, check out your website or bulletin, or corner you after Mass asking about getting married in your church, what is the first response they receive? Here are some we've heard and seen:

- Are you registered in the parish?
- Do you get envelopes?
- You must go through marriage preparation at least six months before your date.
- Here's a brochure with our wedding policies.
- It costs $xxxx.xx to get married in our church.
- You're too late for the class. You'll have to wait until the next class starts.
- Are you baptized?
- Have you been married before?
- I'm too busy right now, but call/e-mail me this week.

The only appropriate first response to couples when they ask about getting married in your church is, "Congratulations! We are so happy for you!" For whatever reason, whether spiritual, practical, or superficial, they have chosen to enter into a committed public union and have chosen your parish to help them do that. Regardless of their reasons, as people of faith, we trust that the Holy Spirit is at work in bringing them to us at this moment in their lives. When we recognize the Spirit at work, our response must be to give thanks and to continue that work begun by the Spirit. All the other details, questions, and policies can come later. But first, we must give that first proclamation of Christ's saving love.

So reexamine your parish's processes for responding to these inquiries. Does the general note in your parish bulletin about weddings or marriage preparation convey the joy of the church for those seeking to be married? Does your parish website immediately show that joy when someone clicks on "Getting Married at St. So-and-So"? Dig up the last e-mail you sent to the mother who asked you about getting her son married in your church. What was the tone of your response? Do your receptionists, secretaries, wedding coordinators, liturgy directors, music directors, and entire parish staff know what their first response to these inquiries should be? (See chapter 11 for an idea on an e-mail response.)

If any of your standard procedures and responses don't communicate that joy right at the start of this couple's inquiry, then change it. Practice it. Make it a priority. That first encounter sets the tone in that couple's mind for what kind of church this will be and what kind of relationship they might desire to have with the Catholic community. This relational first contact then leads naturally into an invitation to one of your parish's marriage discernment gatherings described in the previous section.

If you do this consistently with marriage preparation, it begins to change the culture of the parish so that when others inquire and invite the church to be with them at other significant life events (such as, confirmation, infant baptism, quince años), the automatic, natural response is rejoicing at God's good work in them.

Answering the Telephone

A couple's first direct encounter with a parish representative will likely be with your parish secretary or receptionist. Even if this person is not responsible for taking in the information about the engaged couple when they call or inquire, he or she needs to understand that this first encounter sets the tone for the relationship the parish will build with this couple during their engagement. Here are some tips for that important first conversation:

1. When you know that the persons before you are asking (for themselves or for a friend or relative) about getting married in your parish, be sure that your first response to them is genuine joy and congratulations. This puts them at ease and is basic common courtesy (and good customer service). It lets them know that you do care about them and don't simply see them as an intrusion. And even if it doesn't make any difference to them whether or not you begin this way, it will remind you that they have been loved by God and moved by the Spirit to seek the church's help at this moment in their lives.

2. If they are inquiring about the availability of the church for their wedding date, simply look up the date and let them know whether or not the church might be available. If it is, say that you will pencil in their names but that they will be able to confirm the date after they have met with one of the parish pastoral staff. Above all, do not make any promises regarding the date.

3. Do not rattle off liturgical policies and procedural guidelines during this initial inquiry. But answer any questions they do ask. If they ask for more details on policies and guidelines, refer them to your parish's marriage preparation website or information packet.

4. Take down their names, phone numbers, and e-mail addresses, and let them know that one of the parish's pastoral staff will be in contact with them within forty-eight hours to continue their marriage preparation process. Inform them of any upcoming marriage discernment gathering (see previous section) that might be taking place at your parish (or a neighboring parish).

5. Invite them to come to one of the upcoming Sunday Masses, and let them know who on the parish pastoral staff they can speak with before or after the Mass if they desire to do that.

6. Once you've hung up the phone, immediately relay their contact information and any pertinent questions or unique circumstances you heard from the conversation to the appropriate pastoral staff member. Make a note to follow up with that staff member forty-eight hours later to make sure they had made contact with the couple.

First Interviews

If the parish has been participating in an ongoing proclamation of the love of Christ expressed in the vocation of marriage, the parish staff has been providing opportunities for discernment for this vocation, and the couples who decide to take the next step of formal preparation for marriage are greeted with joy instead of with policies and paperwork, then the initial interviews can be a time to work with each couple to discern their unique path of formation for marriage.

Formation is always about deepening one's relationship with Christ. This relationship presents itself in a person's history and is expressed in that person's desires and hopes for the future. Therefore in these initial interviews, we invite the couples to explore what has been their relationship with Christ in the past, what it is like now, and what they hope for it to be like as married persons in the future. (If a couple had taken part in one of the parish's marriage discernment gatherings, these reflections continue and build upon those discussions.)

These initial interviews with individual couples might be led by one of the parish's pastoral staff or a married couple who has been trained to do the interview process. To help the couple and your pastoral staff prepare a suitable formation, you will be asking the couple to reflect on five questions. Depending on your and the couple's time frame and depth of discussion, you can explore these questions with them over several meetings or during an extended retreat. It is best if each person individually reflects on and writes down his or her own responses. Prior to sharing them with you, they might share their responses with each other. In the first meeting with the couple, present the questions. Explain to them why they are important questions for them to reflect on. Their invitation to the church to witness their marriage shows that they value the role Christ has in their lives. They might not have thought about that role in a while or about the role of faith in their marriage. But as they prepare to commit their lives to one another, Christ and the church will be there to help them in their promises and to strengthen them in their love. Therefore, this is a good time to explore what their relationship with Christ and the church has been like and how they would like to grow in that relationship through their married life together.

Then give them these five faith and marriage questions. Explain that these are questions for each of them to answer individually.

1. Where have I been?
2. Where am I now?
3. Where do I want to get to?
4. How am I going to get there?
5. How will I know that I have arrived?

If the couple is open to beginning the discussion right away, you can help them talk about the first question during that meeting. Or you might invite them to take the questions home and begin to write their own responses to each question.

The goal of these reflections is to draw out each person's narrative of faith and understanding of marriage. This narrative will give you pertinent specific information, such as previous marriages or the presence of children, in such a way that helps them deepen their relationship with Christ. It will also reveal any gaps or even red flags in formation, experience, or understanding regarding discipleship and how that discipleship is lived out in marriage. This will then give you a roadmap for targeted, personalized formation for marriage.

Below are some starter questions for each principle area of discussion. You can give these to them for help in writing their responses, or use them as prompts for group discussion.

1. Where Have I Been?

- When did you first become aware of God?
- Create a faith time line. Indicate the high points in your life when you felt God was really close to you.
- What was your family experience of faith?
- What was your family experience of marriage?
- Did you go to church as a child? as a teenager? as a young adult? How often? What was it like?
- Describe the models of married life you had as a child, teen, and young adult.

- What was your image of God or Jesus as a child? How has that image changed over the course of your life?

- What was your understanding of what marriage is as a child? How has that understanding changed over the course of your life?

- What has happened in your life that has led you to this moment?

2. *Where Am I Now?*

- What is your image of God? What do you believe about God?

- How often are you aware of God in your life? Constantly? Occasionally? Not too much?

- How often do you pray? What is your prayer like?

- How often do you go to church?

- Do you ever talk about God with your fiancé(e)? Describe what that is like.

- What is your relationship with God like right now? Strong or weak? Like a parent and child? Like a good friend? Distant? Close?

- What is your understanding of marriage now?

- What are you most looking forward to in being married?

- What are you most concerned about in being married?

3. *Where Do I Want to Get To?*

- What do you most hope for in your relationship with God?

- What do you most hope for in your marriage?

- Is there someone (or was there someone) in your life you want to be like in regard to faith? to being married? Describe what it is about that person that makes you want to be like him or her.

- Describe how you envision being part of the church community as a married couple.

- Are there any attitudes or behaviors you hope to change in yourself?

- Do you have any hopes for your marriage with regard to faith?

- Is there an area of knowledge you want to strengthen with regard to faith? to marriage?

4. *How Am I Going to Get There?*

- In what ways do you need to develop your faith practices to get to where you want to be?
- In what ways do you need to develop your relationship with your fiancé(e) to get to where you want to be?
- In what ways do you need support from your fiancé(e), family, and friends?
- In what ways do you need support from the faith community at this parish?
- How will you determine if your plan will get you to where you want to be?

5. *How Will I Know That I Have Arrived?*

- How will you know if you have reached your goal?
- How will your fiancé(e), your family, and your friends know you have reached your goal?
- How will the faith community at this parish know if you have reached your goal?

But When Do They Fill Out Paperwork?

Throughout this process, the focus is on the relational aspect of formation rather than solely on protocol and information. Other than specific details, such as name, address, contact information, and birth date, you will get more information by asking these faith questions and listening carefully. Don't be afraid to jot down notes for yourself as the couple talks and shares their responses to these questions. Let them know that you're taking notes in order to help you shape their formation process. You can use your notes to fill out whatever record keeping forms you need to use for each couple.

If you have a standard form that you normally have couples fill out, try holding off on giving them that form until after your first formal meeting with them.

How to Incorporate a Premarital Inventory Tool

There are lots of tools readily available, now many online as well, that you can use to help couples assess their readiness for marriage and pay attention to any areas that need more discussion as they prepare for their wedding. (At foryourmarriage.org, the US Catholic bishops list many of the ones used by Catholic communities in the US, as well as other tools for particular circumstances, such as remarriage, convalidation, and intermarriage.) Inventories like these are great starting points for conversation, but they can never replace a discernment process that includes questions such as those presented above. These premarital inventories also focus mainly on marital issues, as they should. Yet, as a Catholic community, we also want to help our couples focus on their discipleship as Christians and their vocation as married persons with specific roles and gifts to offer the church.

Couples preparing to get married can never have too many tools or methods for getting them to talk more with each other about issues they might not have discussed during their courtship and engagement. So don't think you have to choose either the five faith and marriage questions above or the premarital inventory you already use. Both complement each other.

Most of the premarital inventories use a questionnaire format that asks the person to rank his or her level of agreement to a given statement. Their responses are tallied and scored, showing areas where the couple agrees strongly and other areas where they disagree. Although this report is very useful, the results can sometimes be viewed and discussed in a way that is disconnected from each person's full story, history, and context.

Therefore, one suggestion for using both tools is to begin with numbers 1, 2, and 3 of the faith and marriage questions above, and then use a premarital inventory to discuss very specific points. This gives the couple and those working with them a narrative through which to interpret the results of the inventory. It also builds up the relationship between the partners and between the couple and the one who represents the church community because the "storytelling" aspect of the five questions allows each person to reveal oneself in a way that is more personal, relational, and nuanced.

Preparing a Personalized Formation Plan for Each Couple

Having shared their responses to the first three faith and marriage questions and analyzed and discussed the results from their premarital inventory, now you can all begin to shape a personalized plan of formation that helps each couple strengthen the good things that are already present in their relationship and purify and align the areas where they need the most help.

Do this by having them discuss their responses to questions 4 and 5 above. (It would be most useful to have them write down their responses to all the questions but especially questions 4 and 5.) After they have discussed their responses with you, now you, as their formation guide, have some homework to do. Take their responses from 4 and 5, and, using some of their specific words and phrases, develop a "learning plan" based on the four indispensable tools from chapter 4—Word, community, worship, and witness. See the accompanying learning plan for an example.

Beth and Adam's Marriage Preparation Learning Plan

Beth and Adam's Expectations	The Church's Expectations	Catechism
Beth's goals		
Become more aware of God in my life.	Understand how God is always present in our lives.	1617, 1621, 1659, 1663
Become less judgmental of Adam and others.	Practice Christ's call to unconditional love and sacrifice.	1608, 1642, 1660, 1661
Become friends with other couples at church.	Experience the joy of unity in the Holy Spirit.	1603, 1632, 1658, 1663
Adam's goals		
Become more open to an adult relationship with God.	Understand the commitment to follow Christ.	1621, 1660, 1661

Beth and Adam's Expectations	The Church's Expectations	Catechism
Become less afraid that I will be unfaithful to Beth.	Know and believe in God's faithfulness.	1604, 1608, 1611, 1615, 1661, 1662
With Beth, become good teachers of our faith to our children.	Understand the gifts of the Holy Spirit who gives us wisdom and knowledge.	1632, 1660, 1666
Beth's plan	**A suggested practice**	**A parish activity**
Pray more and be more grateful for my blessings.	Practice daily prayer. Look for daily "God sightings."	Daily Mass Women's group
See the world through the perspective of Adam and my parents.	Deepen compassion and generosity of spirit toward others in need. Practice the church's works of mercy.	Soup kitchen Visit the sick and homebound
Make more time for church.	Participate in a faith-sharing group. Commit to Sunday Mass and staying after Mass to talk to other parishioners.	Renew group Hospitality ministry
Adam's plan	**A suggested practice**	**A parish activity**
Learn to talk to God more.	Pray a daily psalm. Read about the saints.	Men's group
Prioritize my time so that Beth is always my first priority.	Commit to a daily conversation with Beth about where I saw God today. Practice a regular examination of conscience.	Advent retreat Lent retreat
Study about my faith and understand it better.	Participate in a faith-sharing group. Read the *Catechism of the Catholic Church*.	Renew group

The couple's individual responses to number 4 of the faith and marriage questions are summarized in the goals section in this learning plan. The items listed under "The Church's Expectations" is a rewording of these goals in formational language connected to the tradition and practice of the church.

Summaries of each individual's responses to question 5 are listed in the section on each person's plans. In the church's column, give them suggestions for specific Christian practices, habits, and disciplines they can do to put their plan into motion. Be creative and think of a variety of activities and practices they can do individually or together that fall under the formation areas of:

- reflection and study of the Word;
- participation in the community life;
- celebration of the church's liturgies, receiving of blessings, and daily prayer;
- and collaboration with other Christians to witness to the Gospel in their daily lives.

The third column gives some correlations to the Catechism of the Catholic Church that may be used to enhance the formation plan for each individual and ensure a complete preparation for the vocation of marriage. Also listed are specific parish activities that support each person's plan.

Note that not everything in the plan is specifically about preparation for marriage because we are helping the couple deepen their sense of discipleship so that they can exercise their new role as married persons and more committed disciples of Jesus.

Once you have drafted a formation plan for the couple, present it to them and ask them if the goals and plans listed in their column reflect what they had stated in their faith and marriage question responses. Then talk with them about the suggested actions in the church's expectations and activities columns and see if these actions are things they are each willing to try to do during their preparation period. Be flexible and provide alternative actions that might better suit the abilities and resources of the couple. Revise the plan as necessary. Then have each individual make a commitment to that plan. Throughout the next stages of preparation, continually refer back with the couple to this learning plan. If the couple will have a sponsor couple assisting them through the next stage of preparation (see chapter 6), be sure that they also have a copy of this plan so they can help the couple be accountable to their commitment.

6

Apprenticeship in Married Life

The Formation Process

When we are forming catechumens, the church envisions an apprenticeship model of formation:

> The catechumenate . . . is not merely an exposition of dogmatic truths and norms of morality, but a period of formation in the entire christian life, an apprenticeship of suitable duration, during which the disciples will be joined to Christ their teacher. (Decree on the Church's Missionary Activity, 14)

The training is organized around the four categories of Christian life that we discussed in chapter 4. And the training process that we use is one of apprenticeship and mystagogical reflection.

We met some apprentices once. We were visiting a pottery studio, and two pottery students welcomed us. We asked them about the process for learning pottery, and we expected them to tell us something about sitting at the pottery wheel and special techniques they learn to make pots.

Instead, they told us about how they all live together with the master potter and the other pottery apprentices. They eat together and go on outings together too, visiting other studios, learning about the local community, and eating and drinking with these people and seeing how they use pottery in their daily lives. They learn about clay and glazes by finding and collecting the right kind of dirt and plants to use. They learn how to fire their finished pots by exploring the groves around the studio, chopping the wood that will fire the kiln, and stacking that wood in just the right configuration in the kiln. They learn the value of making pots by studying the history of pottery and how pottery has helped to bridge the gap between people of different economic classes and social structures. And they share that value by welcoming visitors, like us, and serving us tea and cookies in cups and plates they have made themselves. They listen to our stories and tell us about their work and why they want to be potters as we all sit around the hearth that stands in the middle of their studio.

As we drank some of their tea, they finally told us about how they learn to make the actual pots. They come to the studio every day and watch the master potter make a pot. Then the master potter gives them a task. Their task that day was to make one hundred of the same pots they saw the master make. We asked them what they did the day before. They made one hundred of the same pots. And what would they make tomorrow? One hundred more pots. We asked them how long they would be making one hundred pots a day. They said until the master potter decides that they are potters.

The apprentices were not yet potters. They looked and acted like potters. They did all the things that potters do. But they had not yet mastered the fundamentals of pottery.

It is probably clear how this story applies to the catechumenate process. When we visited the studio, we were inquirers. The apprentices would be similar to catechumens. And the master potter was the catechist. The studio itself, which served as a hub for the pottery community in that area of the country, would be like the parish.

Here is something that may not be obvious. The main reason the studio exists is not to make pots. The studio exists to make potters. If all of us who are now potters make one hundred pots a day but we don't make any new potters, pottery will die. Our pots may outlive us, but they will eventually break or get lost. The only thing that keeps pottery alive is the creation of new potters.

Likewise, the parish does not exist to teach doctrine. It exists to make disciples. It is the responsibility of every member of the parish to make disciples. And so the central focus of every activity in the parish and the central focus of every parishioner is the catechumenate, which is how we make disciples.

Application to Marriage Preparation

Marriage preparation is also about forming disciples. And the whole parish is responsible for the formation process.

The parish, of course, is already filled with "potters" who are already "making pots." The way they are "making pots" is by living the Christian life within these four categories:

- Word
- Community
- Worship
- Witness

The way we apprentice the engaged couple in this lifestyle is both simple and profound.

The pottery apprentices learned how to make pots by being with the entire community of potters—their master and others skilled in the art, their fellow apprentices, as well as those who visited the studio and those living in the community who use their pottery on a daily basis.

So we also use the entire Christian community to help apprentice engaged couples in living out their baptismal promises in the marriage vocation.

The apprentices and the community also learned by reflecting on their experiences—in formal discussions with their master and other experts and in informal conversation with community members, visitors, and each other.

In the catechumenate, this focused reflection that leads to new learning and conversion is called mystagogy. So we will also use this kind of reflective dialogue to help apprentice the engaged couples in their new lifestyle.

Finally, the master potter didn't just make pots in front of his apprentices and leave them alone to learn for themselves how to be potters. He carefully structured their formation by providing opportunities for the apprentices to be transformed in profound ways from the inside-out into potters. In other words, he introduced them to others who had the heart of a potter so that their own hearts—their internal thoughts, feelings, and attitudes—might grow to become more like that of a true potter and thus transform their external behaviors into genuine actions of a potter.

In any formation process, we call these kinds of moments conversion opportunities in which people meet the risen Christ in a real, personal, and tangible way. It is the Holy Spirit who leads a person to conversion of heart. But we collaborate with the Spirit's work by preparing specific opportunities for that conversion to happen.

In this chapter, we'll look at one specific way the community apprentices engaged couples and how your marriage preparation team can use mystagogy and conversion opportunities to form not only your couples but the entire parish deeper into disciples with the heart of Christ.

Sponsor Couples

With the help of other parishioners, we immerse the couple into parish life. Just as the pottery students were immersed in the entire work of making pots, we immerse the engaged couple in the parish lifestyle activities of Word, community, worship, and witness. One way the parish immerses couples into the married Christian lifestyle is through the guidance of a sponsor couple. Let's look at how we can ask sponsor couples to assist in this.

The RCIA talks about the help and support given to catechumens by "sponsors, godparents, and the entire Christian community" (75.2). In the RCIA, sponsors serve as gifts from the parish given to the person preparing to be baptized. This gift is one of the parish's own who can assist the catechumen in learning about the Christian way of life. Sponsors teach this way of life simply by living out their faith in a visible way for the catechumens so that they can learn by example. Sponsors also talk with the catechumens about their own faith, why they do what they do, how they deal with struggles in their faith, and how they work to strengthen their faith each day.

Being a sponsor is a temporary role that formally begins at the Rite of Acceptance and ends just before the Rite of Election. At that time, the godparent takes over the role of shepherding the catechumen in his or her faith. The godparent is chosen by the catechumen and is a lifetime role. The sponsor and the godparent may be the same person.

How might we use this model of sponsors and godparents in assisting our engaged couples throughout their relationships? Let's focus on the role of sponsor couples who mentor engaged couples in married life.

What Is a Sponsor Couple?

In your parish, there are married couples who are models of the self-sacrificing love of Christ. There are couples who have struggled in their marriage and yet persevere in their promise because of their faith in Christ. There are couples who know what it means to forgive and be forgiven. There are couples who mark five, twenty-five, fifty years or more of married life together and understand the daily commitment to love and serve in the mission of their marriage. Find these couples, and ask them if they would consider becoming a sponsor couple.

Sponsor couples are not marriage counselors. They are mentors and models of healthy (not perfect) Christian marriages. Like the RCIA sponsor, sponsor couples are people who have walked the talk. Their primary role is to serve as an example of what is possible for ordinary Christians who share the same struggles and challenges the engaged couple may face in their own marriage.

Sponsor couples aren't really friends either. Or perhaps it is better to say they are really, really honest friends. Sometimes our friends are not completely honest with us for fear of hurting our feelings. Sponsors are more concerned about our future potential than our feelings. So if something hard needs to be said, a sponsor's job is to say it.

Sponsor couples are also honest about themselves. The best thing a sponsor couple can do is talk about the times they almost didn't make it. They should be completely transparent about their struggles so the engaged couples learn two things: (1) marriage is hard, and (2) even though marriage is hard, there is resurrection. They don't need to simply suffer through hard times, but they do need to stay faithful to get to the joy.

Finally, a sponsor couple needs to be a couple who believes. We tell RCIA sponsors that whatever else they bring to their ministry, they have to bring their faith. It is our faith in Christ that gets us through every hardship and enriches us with every joy. Sponsor couples must go one step further. They have to give witness to faith *as a couple*. We suppose it might be possible for some married couples to have somewhat separate faith lives, but it is not possible for a sponsor couple. We need couples who can show the engaged couples how marriage itself is a spiritual adventure they take together.

What Do Sponsor Couples Do?

Sponsor couples simply spend time with their engaged couples—not in a classroom but in their daily lives where they live out their discipleship through the vocation of marriage.

Here are some general things sponsor couples would do for engaged couples:

- Be with them at Mass on Sunday.
- Invite them into their homes for meals and conversation.
- Pray daily for them.
- Keep in touch with them after the weddings, especially on the newlyweds' anniversaries and other important times of the year.

Now, just as the master potter in our story above showed his students by example not only how to make pots but also how to be potters, sponsor couples would be sure to use the four tools of the parish (see chapter 4) in order to form their engaged couples in the whole lifestyle of being married disciples. Here are ideas on skills for mentoring in the areas of Word, community, worship, and witness.

Mentoring Word Skills

It is important for the sponsor couple to remember they are not catechists. They don't need to "teach" the engaged couple about God's word or church tradition. Instead, their goal is to model how they listen to God's word in their own lives and how they apply church teaching in a way that is fruitful to their marriage. Here are some ways they can do that.

Sponsor couples should be at Mass every Sunday and sit with their engaged couple. After Mass, they all might get together for coffee or brunch. During that social time, the sponsor couple makes sure to ask their engaged couple about what they thought about the homily or something else they saw or heard in the Mass and what it means to them. And if the engaged couple is absent from Sunday Mass, the sponsor couple should show some concern for them, contacting them, letting them know they were missed, and seeing if there is anything they need to help them make their Sunday commitment.

We think it is important the sponsor couples have regular discussions with their engaged couple about how they integrate church teaching into their lives. The sponsors, as we said, are not catechists. They do not need to know all the fine points of what the church teaches in all the areas of faith. They do need to know, however, why they call themselves "Catholic" and how they try to live up to what they believe that means. And, as always, they need to be able to share where they struggle and sometimes fail to live up to their beliefs.

Mentoring Community Skills

The ideal sponsor couple is heavily involved in the parish community. And they should be regularly inviting the engaged couple to join them in the activities of the parish. However, it is important to remember that couples today are often very short on time. So even though invitations should be frequent, there should be some sense of prioritization. What are the engaged couples *welcome* to participate in and what should they be *urged* to participate in? The sponsor couple may need some guidance from the marriage preparation team about this.

One mistake almost every parish makes is they put a lot of emphasis on activities that are happening in the parish buildings. We think it is important, especially for couples learning to become disciples in married life, that the primary emphasis be placed on strengthening the domestic church. So the sponsor couple might ask themselves, What can we do to help the engaged couple learn to establish and solidify Christian community in their own homes now as individuals and in the future as a new family? What did the sponsor couple do when they were engaged and when they became newlyweds? What support did they get or did they wish they had from the parish in building their home life? How can the sponsor couple offer that same support to the engaged couple or how can they alert the parish staff or marriage preparation team to the need for more support for their couple?

Mentoring Prayer and Worship Skills

We have already mentioned how the sponsor couple can assist the engaged couple in participating in Sunday liturgy. In addition, they should also find ways to model a connection with their meals at home and the eucharistic banquet. This can seem difficult, even for long-time Catholics who you might be asking to serve as sponsors. However, it doesn't have to be.

On most nights, especially in families with children, dinner is scattered and rushed. Because that is the most frequent experience of dinner, however, does not mean it should serve as the *normative* experience. Once a week or even once a month the sponsor family should try to have a normal dinner. Normal can mean different things, but here's what we think it means. Everyone in the family is present. Anything with a screen or a ringer is turned off. There is a tablecloth and maybe a candle. The good plates and silverware are used. The meal begins with a prayer. Dessert is a requirement. In other words, dinner should feel elegant. It should feel like a banquet. A normal dinner should be special because the diners are special. To the extent the sponsor couple is able to model this, they should assist the engaged couple in starting their own tradition of normal dining.

The sponsor couple should also assist the engaged couple in developing prayer rituals for their future home together. You can think of lots of examples, and your sponsor couples will also have their own. Here are a few we can suggest. (See also chapter 10 for more ideas and specific prayers.)

- Begin every day with silent prayer and reading Scripture.
- Bless every child before he or she leaves the house.
- Try to read and pray over the Sunday readings before Sunday.
- Conclude every day with the whole family praying the Lord's Prayer.

Mentoring Witness and Service Skills

Here again parishes have a tendency to pull people away from their homes to have them help out at a food shelter or something similar. That's a wonderful instinct, and if couples have the time for it, please make them feel welcome to participate. But we think that for engaged couples, their training in witness and service can begin closer to home.

Almost every family has a ruptured relationship. Ideally, your sponsor couples will have struggled to heal these broken relationships in their own families. They may still be struggling to do so. Their example of their continued, prayerful efforts to remain loving toward difficult family members can be a powerful example for the engaged couples who will be uniting not only themselves but their families together.

Perhaps the most important skill engaged couples can master in this area is sharing faith with each other and others in their households. This is difficult even for lifelong, faithful Catholics. When choosing your sponsor couples, you might want to invite them to share their faith with you and with each other before you pair them with engaged couples. You want to be sure they in fact can share their faith in a meaningful way. We're constantly surprised at the number of Catholics—active parish leaders who are otherwise "picture-perfect" Catholics—who cannot simply talk about their personal belief in Jesus. You will want sponsors who can model this skill for the engaged couples.

How Do You Find Sponsor Couples?

Your staff and marriage preparation team should always keep an eye out for other married couples in the parish who would be good sponsors throughout the year. Think, also, of seeking out married couples who might have the same experiences as your engaged couples, such as, remarriage, ecumenical or interfaith marriage, those who had children before marriage, marriage between two different cultures, or one with a wide age difference.

Each sponsor couple might be given only one or two engaged couples at a time to help shepherd and mentor. Some may want to be connected with more. Each relationship, however, needs to be personal, and the sponsor couple makes a commitment to their couples for at least the duration of their engagement.

Remember, the role of these sponsor couples is temporary, only during the time of the engagement and perhaps to the first anniversary after the wedding. By letting sponsor couples know this up front, they can more readily say yes to your request because it does not need to be a long-term commitment, unless they want it to be.

Twenty Places to Find Sponsor Couples

To be a sponsor couple is to make a big commitment. But believe it or not, there are many people in your parish who are looking to make a big commitment. Sometimes we undersell the commitment people have to make. All that does is say to the volunteer, "I'm not really going to ask very much of you because I don't think you'd really want to do this anyway." Try the opposite. Emphasize the important contribution the sponsor couple *must* make to the lives of the engaged couple and how essential it is to the gospel mission that couples like them make a sacrifice for the sake of the faith. Also, ask the people who are likely to say yes. Here's a list of twenty kinds of couples to ask to be sponsors:

1. Couples who have gone through the RCIA process
2. Couples who were married in your parish five or more years ago
3. The parents of newlyweds
4. The parents of an adult or older child who was recently baptized
5. The parents of the children who have celebrated First Communion within the last five years
6. The parents of teens who were confirmed within the last five years
7. The president of the parish council and his or her spouse (ask six months before the term expires)
8. A Catholic schoolteacher and his or her spouse
9. A newly retired couple
10. The chairperson of last year's banquet committee and his or her spouse
11. All the Communion ministers and their spouses
12. All the lectors and their spouses
13. All the ushers and their spouses
14. All the choir members and their spouses
15. The parish's top ten financial contributors and their spouses

16. All the grandparents of the babies who were recently baptized in your parish

17. All those in the parish who have divorced and remarried

18. The Knights of Columbus and their spouses

19. Anyone who has participated in Cursillo, Renew, Alpha, or another faith-sharing process

20. Anyone who has been an RCIA sponsor and his or her spouse

Mystagogical Reflection

What makes this apprenticeship process into a formation process for discipleship in Christian marriage is mystagogy. Mystagogy is another concept that comes from the Rite of Christian Initiation of Adults. Many of us immediately think of the fifty days of the Easter season, which is identified in the RCIA as the period of mystagogy and postbaptismal catechesis. However, mystagogy is not just a single time frame in the RCIA. Mystagogy is a method of reflecting on and acting on our encounter with the risen Christ.

Therefore, you don't have to wait until after the wedding day to engage in mystagogical reflection with your couples. Inviting your couples to do this kind of reflective thinking and sharing throughout their entire preparation will help them see more clearly God's presence in their daily lives. And when they see that more and more, they will have the hope they will need to be faithful to God and their spouse even in those times when God might feel very absent in their daily lives.

Presumably, if the parish is living out its own discipleship, parishioners are regularly encountering the risen Christ in the four key areas of Christian life: Word, community, worship, and witness. If we immerse the engaged couples in those activities, they too will encounter the risen Christ, and that encounter changes them—but only if they take time to reflect on what happened, what it means, and why it matters. Thus, the mystagogical process, in essence, asks, "So what?" If I truly had an encounter with Christ, what difference does it make in my life?

The marriage preparation team will want to facilitate mystagogical reflection with their engaged couples along with their sponsor couples often during the marriage preparation period, but especially after significant events or moments in the couples' lives or the church community. For example, lead a mystagogical reflection with each of your couples on the event of their engagement. Do mystagogy with all the couples after they were blessed by the parish community at the start of their engagement. Or invite mystagogical reflection on the couples' experience of the feast of the Holy Family, the Easter Sunday Mass, or the parish blessing of anniversary couples.

You can also teach sponsor couples how to lead this kind of discussion on their own so they can do this with their engaged couple at their regular mealtime gatherings.

The mystagogical process has six steps:

1. Encounter
2. Remember
3. Reflect
4. Learn
5. Connect
6. Change

Step 1: Encounter

Sharing faith starts with an event that engages us or makes us feel deep emotion. Family reunions, Easter dinner, graduation, a child's birth, a friend's death, the shared experience of watching a movie or hearing a song—all these are ripe with moments in which the mystery of faith can be uncovered. As you are participating in the life of faith, notice these profound moments of encounter with Christ. During these moments, pay close attention to all your senses (what you see, hear, touch, taste, smell) and to what you feel. Engage fully in the experience.

Step 2: Remember What Happened

After the event, gather with others who experienced the same thing. Ask these questions: What did you see? What did you hear? What do you remember most? Be very concrete in your memories. For example, "When I went home for Thanksgiving, I smelled bread baking when I came in the door, and was welcomed in by my brother, who gave me a big hug because we haven't seen each other in a long time. It's the first Thanksgiving after we lost our Mom, and now it's just us in the family. My brother had a bunch of his friends there too, and they also welcomed me with hugs."

Step 3: Reflect on the Bigger Picture

In this step, ask how this experience made you feel and what this experience means to you. For example, "That smell of bread and seeing my big brother reminded me of my childhood when I felt so cared for and like everything was right. It was the smell of being home, and I felt that I belonged there. Fresh baked bread always meant that something special was happening in our family."

Step 4: Learn about Our Faith

In this step, ask what this memory teaches you about God, about Christ, about church, about community. For example, "My feeling of belonging when I smelled that bread baking teaches me that family can be anyone I share food with. It reminds me of all those Bible stories of Jesus eating meals with others and how we share bread and wine with strangers at Mass every Sunday. These strangers we call brothers and sisters because we eat together. It teaches me that no matter what, I can depend on my family, my community." Find out what the church teaches about your insight. Connect it to a story in the Bible, and find out what Scripture teaches about this.

Step 5: Connect with Your Life

What else is going on in your life that needs to be connected to this concrete experience and memory? What issues is the couple dealing with? What concerns do they have in their daily lives? What are some major events happening in your community or in the world? For example, "That smell of bread baking makes me think of my future family and how I worry about making sure they have enough to eat. I worry about my job and if I'll still have it next month. I think also of the man I see every morning on the street corner asking for money for food."

Step 6: Make a Change

This is the "so-what" step. What will you do differently in your life now that you've made these connections with your faith? Perhaps the couple might decide to participate in Communion with different eyes, really looking at each person in the Communion procession as family. Maybe they will choose to begin each dinner with a simple prayer. They might become more aware of issues of homelessness and hunger. They might become more interested in parish-led efforts to assist those who are homeless or hungry, or who have lost jobs or are looking for work.

This six-step process repeats continuously, just as the pottery apprentices continued to make one hundred pots every day. The doing of Christian life is what makes disciples, just as molding clay into pots makes potters.

Conversion

You will recall that in chapter 2 we said that conversion is job one in the initiation process. It is also job one in the marriage preparation process. Conversion has to precede everything we do in marriage preparation because we are not just preparing two people to be husband and wife. We are preparing them to be *disciples as husband and wife*. If they have not yet truly encountered the risen Christ in their lives, we have to introduce them before we can go one step further.

The *General Directory for Catechesis*[1] speaks quite strongly about this:

> Many who present themselves for catechesis truly require genuine conversion. Because of this the Church usually desires that the first stage in the catechetical process be dedicated to ensuring conversion. . . . Only by starting with conversion . . . can catechesis, strictly speaking, fulfill its proper task. (62)

The emphasis on new evangelization in the last decade has reminded us that baptism and even active church life are no guarantees of conversion. We cannot assume that those who come to us for marriage preparation—even if they are baptized and even if they are active parishioners—are living the life of discipleship.

So here's the rub. If a couple wants to get married, and the first thing we do is pull down a marriage preparation program off the shelf and start at page 1, we're probably not going to have much impact on the faith lives of the couple. There are a lot of great marriage prep programs out there, and there is absolutely a place for them in your preparation process. But you have to *start* with conversion.

How to Encounter the Risen Christ

For those of us who do have an active, personal relationship with Jesus, it seems astounding that we have to even think about how to *provide* an encounter with the risen Christ. We encounter Jesus at every waking moment—and even in our dreams sometimes. But for many people, even active Catholics, they not only don't know how to have a personal relationship with Jesus but they actually may think it is not even possible.

Now we all know that we, all by ourselves, cannot cause conversion. Faith is a gift of the Holy Spirit, not of us. However—and this is a big "however"—the Spirit works through us. So we have a definite role to play. There are measurable, specific things we can do to provide *opportunities* for conversion. And, as we said, we have to do these things before we can start doing the more traditional types of formation. So here are some principles.

Conversion Is Communal

Conversion usually happens amidst a group of disciples, sharing faith through actions or words. Some people travel to a mountaintop or see an ocean sunset and are converted to Christ. But that's not usual. Conversion usually happens when a group of disciples do stuff or say stuff that makes it clear to the unconverted that Jesus makes a difference.

Conversion opportunity 1: Schedule time to talk about your faith with the engaged couple. Talk about all the ways Jesus makes a real difference in your life. Be sure to talk about the person of Jesus Christ—not just "the church" or "the faith." Schedule time for the sponsor couple and other parishioners to also share their faith with the couple. If possible, schedule time for the pastor to share his faith as well.

Conversion Is Liturgical

As Catholics, we believe the fullest encounter with the risen Christ that we can have is in the liturgy. Sunday liturgy is the paramount encounter, but all liturgy is an encounter with the real presence of Jesus Christ.

Conversion opportunity 2: Schedule regular times for couples to participate in both parish liturgies and domestic church liturgies. Provide ways for them to reflect mystagogically on those encounters with the risen Christ.

Conversion Is Situational

The Holy Spirit does not just throw a big blanket of conversion over the world and expect us all to get it. Conversion happens in each individual heart, and the day-to-day encounters with Christ that are unique to each of us draw us closer to union with Christ. It is the specific situation of each person's life that is the "map" of conversion.

Conversion opportunity 3: Schedule regular times for discussions about the daily life events of the couple. These can be discussions with you, with their sponsor couple, with their parents, or just with each other. The focus of these discussions is always some version of "Where did you see God today?"

Conversion Happens When We Encounter the Poor

When we meet the poor and rejected and learn to love them, we are changed, just as Jesus was changed. Jesus so loved and identified with the poor that the church teaches that when we encounter a poor person (or a sick person, a prisoner, an addict, or anyone "on the margins"), we are meeting Christ face-to-face.

Conversion opportunity 4: Schedule regular times for couples to interact with people on the margins of society. This could be a regular ministry your parish already engages in. It could also be asking the couples to reach out to estranged members of their families. Or it could be offering support to someone who is being discriminated against in his or her workplace or neighborhood.

Conversion Is Intentional

Conversion happens when we ask for it to happen. No prayer ever goes unheeded, especially a prayer for faith. Sometimes, if someone is struggling with a lack of belief, we have to offer a very small step toward the risen Christ. Perhaps his or her prayer is simply "Help me to pray" or "Help me to see."

Conversion opportunity 5: Provide regular times for prayer to ask for deeper faith. Provide days of reflection, tools for a daily examination of conscience, retreats, reading materials, and anything else you can imagine that will stimulate the couple's reflection on faith.

If we apprentice our engaged couples by using the community as the models of disciples, inviting them to mystagogical reflection on their encounter with Christ in the big and small events of their daily lives, and by providing them with conversion opportunities to meet the risen Christ, we will have couples who are not only ready to be married but are ready to live out their Christian faith as husbands and wives.

Once your couple has reached this level of discipleship in marriage, they are ready to enter into the final period of preparation for their wedding.

Spiritual Preparation for the Rite

*I*n the catechumenate process, there is a time of more intense spiritual preparation for the celebration of the initiation rites. This is called the period of purification and enlightenment and usually coincides with the forty days of Lent.

This is a period that is unique to unbaptized people preparing for initiation. There is no similar period for baptized candidates who are preparing to either complete their initiation or to be received into the full communion of the Catholic Church. Therefore, some of the elements of the period of purification and enlightenment will not exactly translate to the marriage preparation process. Nevertheless, if we can uncover the underlying principles of this period, we can find some useful guidance for enhancing the spiritual preparation of couples preparing for marriage.

Intense Spiritual Preparation

The period of purification and enlightenment is, for the catechumens, "a period of more intense spiritual preparation, consisting more in interior reflection than in catechetical instruction" (RCIA, 139). If you think of a runner on the day before the big race, the period of purification and enlightenment is something like that day. All the training is complete, and now the runner's job is to get spiritually and mentally ready for the big event.

For the catechumen, this intense spiritual preparation happens in several ways:

- Public commitment
- Liturgical prayer

- Personal prayer
- Spiritual recollection
- Penitential practice

Let's look at the journey of the engaged couple and apply some principles of this part of the initiation process to the marriage preparation process.

Betrothal

"Betrothal" is an old-fashioned word that isn't used much anymore. Couples more often speak of "engagement." And you should probably stick with that word when you are talking with them. But just between us, "betrothal" connotes a richer, deeper process of commitment that is a closer parallel to the catechumenate process.

As you probably know, a *betrothal* is the giving of one's troth. That is, it is the giving of one's true promise. The betrothal is somewhat akin to the public commitment the catechumens make at the beginning of the period of purification and enlightenment. For the catechumens, that commitment takes place at the Rite of Election, during which the catechumens are formally chosen or "elected" for initiation at the next Easter Vigil. It is a covenant entered into by both the catechumen and the church. And as soon as the catechumens make that public commitment, they are given a new name. They are now called "elect."

A betrothal is also a public commitment that changes the status of the couple. And they are also usually called by a new name—fiancées. Usually, a betrothal is not public in the liturgical sense. That is, couples usually get engaged in private or at least outside of the church. Parish leaders could provide a ritual that brings the couple's engagement into the heart of the worshiping assembly. The *Book of Blessings*, for example, supplies an "Order of Blessing an Engaged Couple." (This also appears in the appendix of the Order of Celebrating Marriage.) We have seen this rite celebrated at a Sunday Mass with all the couples of the parish who are planning to be married in the near future—say, three to six months.

Unlike catechumens who usually come to us as mere inquirers, couples come to us having already "given their troth." So their actual engagement cannot serve as the beginning of a more intense spiritual preparation for the marriage preparation process. But you could use the *blessing* of their engagement as such a marker. At an appropriate time, when you believe couples are adequately prepared for the promises that will be asked of them in the wedding rite (see chapter 9: Three Steps to Know If a Couple Is Ready for Marriage), you could celebrate a public blessing that would begin a period of spiritual preparation for them.

Engagement

"In the United States couples in the past often have requested a simple blessing upon the recently given or received engagement ring. Very few, however, ask for a formal betrothal or engagement ceremony. Nevertheless, couples from Hispanic tradition frequently observe a series of ritualized customs connected with the prospective bride and groom's request for engagement.

"While there are good reasons for encouraging an integration of the couple's religious practices and their nuptial engagement, the American bishops have emphasized that the freedom and even responsibility of either person or both to terminate the engagement and not proceed with the marriage must always be taught and fostered" ("Marriage, Liturgy of," in *The New Dictionary of Sacramental Worship*, ed. Peter E. Fink, 798–99 [Collegeville, MN: Liturgical Press, 1990]).

Strengthening

During the period of purification and enlightenment, the elect celebrate three scrutiny rites. The purpose of these rites is "to uncover, then heal all that is weak, defective, or sinful in the hearts of the elect; to bring out, then strengthen all that is upright, strong, and good" (RCIA, 141).

Here again, we must point out that scrutinies are unique to the unbaptized. We cannot, nor would we want to, celebrate scrutinies or anything like scrutinies with engaged couples. However, we might want to provide ways that they can uncover any lingering resistance, weakness, or fear that might still be in their hearts. And we would certainly want to give them all the help we can in strengthening the love, goodness, friendship, and grace that is growing between the two of them.

One simple way to accomplish this is by praying the Lord's Prayer. The Lord's Prayer is something of an *examen* ("forgive us our sins, as we forgive . . ."). And it is also a prayer for strength ("Give us this day our daily bread"). Presumably you have been providing the engaged couple with prayer suggestions and opportunities throughout the preparation process (see chapter 10). Here, in this more intense period of preparation, we are suggesting you turn it up a notch. Ask the couple to commit to praying the Lord's Prayer at the three principle hours of the day—morning, noon, and night. Ideally, they would do this together, but at least on their own if that isn't possible.

This seems like a simple, unobtrusive spiritual practice to add into their daily routine. But try it yourself for thirty days. It takes some discipline and conscious effort to keep up the practice. And that's the point. By committing to each other and to the parish that they will practice this discipline for the time just before their marriage, the couple will uncover and heal all that is weak within them and likewise strengthen all that is good and holy.

Reconciliation

If your marriage preparation has been a true conversion process, the engaged couples will discover the necessity to change—to convert from a former way of life to a new way of life in Christ. Some of the couples will, no doubt, already be living a Christian lifestyle, perhaps an exemplary one. But all of us, especially when we come to transition moments in our lives, realize we have fallen short of the fullness a life in Christ offers us.

In the language of the catechumenate, the tendency to hang on to a way of life we have rejected is called "the mystery of sin" (RCIA, 143). Even our greatest saints become ensnared in this mystery. Saint Paul writes about "a thorn in the flesh," a "[messenger] of Satan," that continually torments him (2 Cor 12:7). All of us suffer from temptations and torments that can separate us from God's love.

Sadly, a common thorn for many young people is that they may never have experienced unconditional love in their lives. We rejoice with them that they have finally found that love in each other, and we hope that our conversion-focused marriage preparation process has helped them recognize God's unconditional love for them.

But like St. Paul's thorn, their lifelong experience of alienation may still ensnare them. This dynamic often happens with catechumens. They are fascinated by the love of God, and at the same time they are bound by a lifetime of behaviors that have protected them from too much pain or loneliness.

For the unbaptized, we pray exorcisms over them to free them from the "messengers of Satan" that keep them bound. For Christians, we celebrate the sacrament of penance to reconcile to God's love and to remind us we are no longer captives to the mystery of sin.

As engaged couples come closer to the celebration of their marriage, we can help free them from the entanglements of a previous lifestyle of alienation and loneliness by celebrating a fruitful sacramental reconciliation with them.

Retreats

Your parish or your diocese probably already asks engaged couples to make a retreat before their marriage. We think it's important to ask why we do this. If you ask people why they go on retreats, you'll get many answers. To renew, refresh, get away, pray, connect, rest, grow, and more. All of these are terrific benefits of retreats.

In the catechumenate, however, there is an overarching purpose for a retreat—to deepen the conversion of the catechumen to Christ. We think that whatever other benefits a retreat for engaged couples provides, this should be the number one purpose.

Turning to Christ in such a deep and powerful way is not always natural for us. The thorn of temptation that St. Paul writes about, as well as just the mad dash of daily life, distract us from the small quiet sound of God's Spirit. But when we step away from it all for just a bit and really listen, God's voice becomes so resonant and clear. We feel God's Spirit well up within us and fill us with love and power.

Too often, however, the retreats that we prepare for engaged couples focus mainly on their relationship with each other and try to work through many of the issues that should have already come up in their preparation long before the retreat. The retreat itself, especially if it comes toward the end of the engagement, should indeed be a retreat and not an extended class or workshop. One benefit to doing a marriage preparation process that is truly gradual in nature and focused on conversion is that the retreat can become an intense and focused spiritual deepening of the couple's relationship with Christ, since the major issues about marriage have already been discussed and examined through the numerous conversations with their sponsor couple, the discernment evenings throughout the year, the workshops on communication and other practical issues of living with another person, the regular journaling and intimate sharing of their reflections, and the one-on-one meetings with a pastoral minister. But if these other formational moments have not happened throughout the entire preparation period, it is no wonder, then, that we try to cram all of it into the day or weekend of a retreat.

A retreat doesn't have to be lengthy, but it does have to be focused. It should probably be away from home and perhaps even away from the parish. It can be a single day, or a weekend, or a week. If you already have a retreat as part of your marriage preparation process, evaluate it to see how well you believe it focuses on conversion. A retreat usually is not a time for catechesis or information delivery. It is a time for prayerful listening.

We suggest three retreat opportunities, if possible. One might take place just before you begin formal preparation with the couple. This would be similar to the inquirers spending focused prayer time with the RCIA team to discern their readiness for entering the catechumenate. This first retreat might be structured around the three questions of the marriage rite (see chapter 2: Why Is Conversion Important?).

The second retreat opportunity might take place a month or two before the wedding and would be parallel to the catechumens going on retreat to discern if they are ready to celebrate the Rite of Election and begin their final spiritual preparation for initiation. Here, you might focus on the primary symbols of the rite, including the readings the couple has chosen. You might also ask the couple to reflect again on the three questions they discussed at their first retreat to see how much they have grown in their relationship with Christ and each other.

As a conclusion to this retreat, you might "present" the wedding vows to the couple, in a similar way that we present the Lord's Prayer and the Creed to the elect in the RCIA. The point of presenting the vows to the couple is to invite them to use these words as a daily meditation during the final months of their engagement. The couple would also be encouraged to use their daily reflection on the vows as a way to memorize them so that they can speak these vows from their heart on the day of their wedding.

This ritual presentation might be led by the couple's sponsor couple who has walked with them throughout their engagement or, if they have chosen one, the couple who will serve as their mentors during their married life. See the sidebar for a sample outline of this presentation.

Outline for Presenting the Vows

Opening Song

Reading

Use one of the readings that will be proclaimed at the couple's wedding.

Reflection

The members of the marriage preparation team and the sponsor couple might say a few words of encouragement for the engaged couple, naming how they have seen God working in their lives over the course of their engagement.

Presentation

The sponsor couple invites the engaged couple to stand. All who are married then stand around them in a circle facing the engaged couple.

Sponsor couple:
"N. and N., listen now to the words of the vows you will make at the end of your engagement and the beginning of your vocation to the married life. Receive them now with an open heart, meditate upon them in the days to come, and strive to always be faithful to them for ever."

Married couples only speak these words slowly, pausing at the end of each line:

   (Men) "I take you to be my wife."
   (Women) "I take you to be my husband."
   (Together) "I promise to be faithful to you,

in good times and in bad,
in sickness and in health,
to love you and to honor you
all the days of my life."

Prayer

Use one of the prayers from the Order of Blessing an Engaged Couple
or another suitable prayer.

Sign of Peace

The third and last retreat before the wedding also has a parallel
with the catechumenate. On Holy Saturday, the elect spend the day
in prayer and preparation for their initiation that night. Imagine inviting the couple, their families, and wedding party to spend a couple
of hours on retreat on the day of the wedding rehearsal. Instead of
letting this day descend into a dizzying whirlwind of last-minute
activities, you actually might be able to give them the great gift of
peace, reflection, and prayer that helps them face the upcoming day.
We have heard so many couples bemoan the fact that they had let the
stress of the wedding day activities overtake them so they could not
enjoy any minute of it—or the days after. (One newlywed actually
said that his new bride was so exhausted from all the planning and
preparation that she slept through the wedding night and the first
few days of their honeymoon!) The third retreat opportunity might
be the most difficult one to do, but it may be the most needed.

If you do decide to keep the wedding rehearsal day as a day of
retreat, consider providing some simple rituals and practices that give
a bit of structure to the day. Here are some possibilities.

Fasting

In the catechumenate, the elect are asked to fast on Good Friday and
Holy Saturday. When we are explaining the fast, we tell them that
this is a "paschal fast" and not a "penitential fast." What's a paschal
fast? they will usually ask. And we tell them it is similar to a bride

or groom being too nervous to eat before the wedding. It is a fast of anticipation and joy.

And now, we will flip that and say that the paschal fast for a bride and groom is like the fast of the elect before their initiation. It is a fast of preparation for the important life-changing event they are about to celebrate. As you know, the fasting rules for Catholics are not very strict. On fast days, we only eat one regular meal and we may eat two smaller meals that are more like large snacks. And we avoid eating between meals. The point is not so much about the quantity of food. It is about changing the way we eat to remind us we are about to change the way we live. Even if you are not able to provide a retreat for your engaged couples, do encourage them to fast either on the days leading up to their rehearsal day or their wedding day or on those days themselves. The rehearsal dinner and the wedding dinner can serve as the end of the fast.

Vows

On the Holy Saturday retreat day, the elect are asked to recite the Creed. The Creed was presented to them earlier in Lent as one of the treasures of the church for them to hold in their hearts. They are asked to memorize it and return it back to the community on Holy Saturday. They will say the Creed again—in the form of baptismal promises—later that night at the Easter Vigil.

As a parallel to this, you could create a simple prayer service in which the couple rehearses their wedding vows for the parish community. You don't need the whole parish there. Family, a few friends, sponsor couples, and the wedding party are enough. By first giving their vows to the community before they give them to each other, they are announcing to the community that these are the promises they intend to make. Also, if you ask the couples to memorize their vows—just as the elect are to memorize the Creed—they are demonstrating to the community that they have taken these vows to heart.

A New Name

The elect are not asked to take on baptismal names, even if their given names are not "Christian." They are baptized with the names they grew up with. Even so, the RCIA includes a ritual for the giving of a new name for use in countries where it is a cultural tradition to take on a new name or where someone may have a name that is antithetical to the gospel. In the United States, many parishes adapt this ritual into a blessing of the given names of the elect—the names they grew up with and with which they will be baptized.

In most marriages, the bride takes on a new name—her husband's family name. We think it could be another moment of conversion to provide a prayerful setting in which both the bride and groom talk about their family names and what those names mean to them. If the bride is taking on her husband's name, provide a way for her to say good-bye to her old name and speak about what she looks forward to as she takes on her new name.

For couples who are keeping their original names (or those who are combining their names), you could still create a prayer in which they reflect on what it will be like to take on the names of "husband" and "wife." You could also have them reflect on their individual family names and what it will be like for their two family names to be united into one household.

Rehearsal

When we rehearse the RCIA rituals, including initiation, the catechumens are not present. We ask sponsors and perhaps family to be at the rehearsal to learn where the catechumens have to be at each point in the rite. We do not want the catechumens worrying about what's next and if they are going to be in the right spot at the right time and say the right thing. We put all this burden on the sponsors so the catechumens can stay focused on how Christ is speaking to them in the rite.

It isn't feasible to absent the bride and groom from the wedding rehearsal. However, the principle should remain the same. We want to relieve the bride and groom of as much worry and detail as possible so they can focus on the voice of Christ in the sacramental moment.

Every couple is different, of course, and some couples may be more anxious or distracted than others. Trying to create an atmosphere of calm, let alone prayerful attention to God's Spirit, may be beyond possibility in some cases. Even so, if we bring this hope to the wedding rehearsal along with some pastoral strategies that allow for the possibility, many couples will likely take advantage of the opportunity and be grateful for a moment of calm in the excitement of preparations.

You can find a prayer for beginning the wedding rehearsal in chapter 10. Also, many wedding liturgy resources provide prayer suggestions for beginning a rehearsal. We suggest you use one of these to create a prayer that is somewhat formal without being stuffy. By beginning with a prayer that takes a bit of preparation and attention, you will help all those gathered to enter into a time out of time—a holy moment.

One idea that some pastors have used successfully is to celebrate the Liturgy of the Hours (Evening Prayer) with the entire wedding party at the beginning of the rehearsal. This does several things: it puts the entire gathering in an atmosphere of prayer; it introduces family and friends who might not be familiar with communal prayer to a simple, full, and accessible liturgy; and it ensures that the rehearsal will not begin until everyone is present.

Another pastoral tactic is to be sure the sponsor couple knows the ritual inside and out. As you lead the wedding party through the steps of the liturgy, the sponsor couple can place a gentle hand on the arm of a wandering groomsman or field a whispered question from a nervous bridesmaid while you keep the flow of the rehearsal moving smoothly.

The most important thing to communicate to the couple is that it is impossible for them to make a mistake in the liturgy. Relieve them of the fear that they have to remember everything. Assure them over and over again that you, the sponsor couple, the wedding coordinator, and the musician are all going to make sure the wedding will go off without a hitch. It is your job—the religious professionals—to make sure things are right. The bride and groom should focus on how God is speaking to them on their wedding day. They should let you worry about the technical details.

It is also helpful and a way of spiritually preparing the entire wedding party to focus less on the dos and don'ts of the wedding rite and more on the meaning behind what we do in the ritual. Why is it important that we not chew gum in church? What makes this space different than other places where we gather? What does it mean to have all these bridesmaids and groomsmen standing by the couple? What is their spiritual role in the rite? People are more likely to honor the dos and don'ts if they understand why they are important and meaningful to the event.

Finally, conclude the rehearsal with a blessing of the couple. We suggest this blessing include a physical laying on of hands on the heads of both the bride and the groom. You lead and model the action, and then invite each member of the wedding party to do the same. This is a powerful, prayerful action that draws even the most spiritually dormant member of the group into a moment of prayer and contemplation.

8

Postsacramental Reflection

*B*eing married is hard work. If you are married, you know this. If you are newly married, you may have made an intellectual assent to this notion, but you can't ever really know how hard it is until you've done it. The simple fact is, no matter how well we prepare couples, the day is going to come when they are stuck in a cold, silent place in their marriage, scared to death that they may not be able to fix it. As Christian communities, we have to be ready to help them on that day.

To do that, we have to maintain an active relationship with newly married couples, especially throughout the first year of their marriage. This is similar to the church's strategy for the neophytes. The US bishops have asked that we consider the newly baptized to be neophytes until the first anniversary of their initiation. A "neophyte" is a "new plant." It has roots, but it is still young and vulnerable to being uprooted by bad weather and outside forces. The job of the parish is to provide regular gatherings and ongoing support for the neophytes so they will weather the storms that will surely come and will not waver in their faith.

Couldn't we apply that same idea to newlyweds? What if we considered newlyweds to be "neophyte couples" for the first year of their marriage? Of course, they are different than baptismal neophytes. We can imagine saying to a baptismal neophyte, "We're here for you when your faith journey gets difficult and you are struggling with staying true to your baptismal promises." It seems less acceptable to say to newlyweds, enraptured in love, "We're here for you when your marriage hits a rough patch and you are struggling to stay true to your marriage vows." And yet, we have to find accessible ways to offer exactly that kind of support. We really believe that if married couples who have been through it can be available to newlyweds who are challenged by starting a new life together, perhaps having their first child and needing to learn entirely new coping skills to get through each day, we would go a long way toward reducing the number of marriages that fail.

A marriage doesn't usually fail because of one or two bumps in the road. The failure is when those bumps are not negotiated well and a destructive pattern develops that makes all further bumps bigger and more dangerous. If experienced couples could help by offering skills for getting through the difficulties (and for savoring the joys), the newlyweds will learn how to find their way along the path of marriage. And then the newlyweds, having learned how to grow strong in their faith and in their marriage, will in turn become a source of strength for future newlyweds in the community.

Beyond failure, however, is also the fact that the church made a commitment to the couple. When we stood as witness to their vows, we made a commitment—as profound as the vows the couple made to each other—to support them in their vocation. Our commitment to this couple did not end with the end of the wedding; it was only just beginning.

Mystagogy

In the RCIA, the final stage in the conversion process is called the period of postbaptismal catechesis or mystagogy. This period "is a time for the community and the neophytes together to grow in deepening their grasp of the paschal mystery and in making it part of their lives through

> meditation on the Gospel,
> sharing in the eucharist,
> and doing the works of charity." (RCIA, 244)

All of us who are baptized are in this period of postbaptismal catechesis. All of us are called to continually deepen our grasp of the paschal mystery and to reflect on the Word, celebrate the Eucharist, and go out in mission to serve those in need. The purpose of doing this for the neophytes is to help them see the world in a different way—through the lens of the sacraments they have celebrated. With newlyweds, we can help them see their world and their role in it through the lens of the marriage vows they have made. This lens, as it is with all sacraments, is a way of seeing life through the power of the paschal mystery: where giving ourselves completely means finding our true selves whole again; where laying down our life for another means receiving a new life that is more wondrous than we could imagine; where darkness and death are opportunities for the God of light and life to work through us to bring healing and hope.

The principal way we help neophytes do this is through their "personal experience of the sacraments and of the community" (RCIA, 247) in the vibrant celebration of the Sunday Eucharist, especially those immediately following their initiation.

We can do something similar with the newlyweds after their sacrament of matrimony. On the Sundays after their wedding, you might continue to gather with them (as you had been during their preparation process) during the first six months of their marriage for perhaps three formal sessions of mystagogy.

We've talked about mystagogy already in chapter 6. In that chapter, we gave you a six-step outline for doing a mystagogical reflection on a significant experience the couple has had. This experience may or may not have been a liturgy or even a particularly religious experience, but it did give them an encounter with the risen Christ in some way.

In this chapter, we'll give you a similar process to do mystagogical reflection with the couples specifically on the marriage rite itself. As Catholics, we believe that our premier encounter with Christ is in the sacraments when the church gathers to give praise to the Father and be transformed by the Spirit. For these sessions, it might be helpful to have assistance from one of your catechists or pastoral staff persons.

After the Sunday Mass, gather with the newlyweds and any of their family members, friends, or sponsor couples who were also with them on the day of their wedding. Be sure to allow for socializing with the parish community if there is a coffee and donut gathering after Mass.

Prepare a quiet, prayerful space for the gathering, with comfortable chairs set in a circle around a prayer focal point. This prayer table might include a Lectionary or Bible, a lit candle, a cross, and, if you have them available, some wedding symbols, such as a veil and rings. You might even have some cupcakes set on the table as a reminder of the wedding cake they shared (be sure to have enough cupcakes to share with everyone after the session!). Have some quiet instrumental music playing as well.

If there are several couples gathering together, be sure all have name tags and have time to introduce themselves to the group.

For the first session, you might want to describe a little bit of what you will be doing with them during the next hour. Let them know that you will lead them all in a prayerful remembering of their wedding day. Their memories will then be the starting point for talking about how they have grown in their love for one another and for Christ and in their understanding of their marriage vocation.

The following six steps are very similar to those outlined in chapter 6. Here we will give a bit more detail for each step:

1. Liturgy (encounter with God)—about 5 minutes

   Here, invite the participants to close their eyes and recall back to the day of the wedding. Ask them to remember some of the specific things from that day. You might prompt them with phrases such as these:

   a. Remember seeing the church.

   b. (To the newlyweds) Remember seeing each other for the first time.

   c. Remember the moment of the vows.

   d. Remember the rings.

   e. Remember how you felt.

   Let this be a quiet time for them to remember in their mind's eye what they had experienced that day in their particular roles. After some time, invite everyone to open their eyes.

2. Recollection (of the liturgy's symbols, actions, texts)—10 minutes

   Give the entire group a few minutes now to share with another person some of their memories of the wedding day. After a few minutes, gather the group's attention again and, starting with the newlyweds, ask them to share with the entire group some of their memories from the wedding liturgy. Encourage them to be specific about their memories. For example, if someone says, "I was just so happy the entire time," ask, "Was there one specific moment that you remember that made you feel so happy? What was happening in the liturgy at that moment? What did you see, hear, or do that made you feel so happy?"

Help them keep their memories to the liturgy itself. Be sure that everyone among the newlyweds who wants to talk has a chance to share his or her memories. Then invite any of the family or friends present to do the same.

3. Reflection (on what was most memorable)—10 minutes

Now ask each person to quietly think of his or her most memorable moment from the wedding liturgy. For those who like to write down their thoughts, you might invite them to write down this memory on paper. Again, ask them to be specific, using these three questions:

a. What did you see, hear, or do in that moment that made it so memorable for you?

b. How did that make you feel?

c. What did that moment mean to you? Did it say something to you about God? about Christian love? about commitment? about promises? about yourself as a disciple?

After a minute or so of quiet reflection, invite some people to share out loud their most memorable moment. Be sure to give the newlyweds priority in the sharing. Make note of any reflections that are powerful for the group or seem to be a memory shared by many in the group.

4. Catechesis (connecting to Scripture and tradition)—15 minutes

Take one of the memories that was shared in the previous step (the one that moved the entire group or was widely shared among them), and begin making some connections to our Scriptures and tradition.

For example, if the memory you chose to focus on was the newlyweds' experience of exchanging rings, you might talk about how in the Scriptures, there are many references to jewelry—physical jewels that people would wear or give to one another. But the Scriptures also talk about how the people who belong to God are like a bride adorned with jewels, beautiful in the eyes of God. In a similar poetic way, the temple of the New Jerusalem is adorned with gold and precious jewels signifying the beauty of the way of life of those who follow the way of Jesus.

However, we also know the story of the Israelites who wandered in the desert for forty years. When they felt lost as if God had abandoned them, they gathered up all their gold, including all the golden rings they wore, melted them down, and created their own god because they had lost faith in the God who led them out of slavery.

Several other examples show us another meaning of rings. When the prodigal son returns home to his father, the father welcomes him with open arms and lavish gifts. He puts the finest robe on his son and a ring on his finger to express the reconciliation that the father offers to his son who had been lost.

The Scriptures and our Christian tradition also give importance to the wearing of rings. In the Bible, signet rings were often used to identify a person as belonging to a particular household or being an official representative of that family, whether by blood or friendship. Bishops and religious brothers and sisters are also often given rings to wear after they have made their vows to live out their vocation.

Ask the group what they think the giving and receiving of rings between husband and wife means based on all these other connections. Do they have any new insights about what the newlyweds did in that exchange of rings that tells them something new about Christian marriage? Affirm any points they make that support our Christian teaching, redirect any ideas that go astray, and fill in any significant gaps that may be missing in their reflection.

5. Connection (to one's life)—10 minutes

Now ask the group to reflect quietly on what is going on in their own lives, in their relationships with others, or in the world right now that might need to hear the insights that have been uncovered in this discussion. Give some quiet time for them to reflect on their own or to write down their thoughts. Then invite them to share with another person.

After a few moments, invite those who would like to share their thoughts with the group.

6. Conversion (why it matters)—10 minutes

The last step is to invite all in the group to make a commitment in their life of faith based on today's reflection. What is one thing they are willing to do this week to live out more deeply the promises of faith they have made to God, to another person, or to their family and community? Invite any who would like to share with the group. Be sure to make your own commitment as well. Conclude the gathering by praying together the Lord's Prayer or another prayer over the group.

Keep the Relationship Going

In the catechumenate, we recommend monthly gatherings of the neophytes throughout the first year after their baptism. Once the formal mystagogy sessions above are completed, consider an informal gathering every three months with all the newlyweds from the parish. This should be mostly a social event, but always begin with prayer. Invite the couples to bring photos from their wedding and any trips or events they have been on recently.

While you want these gatherings to be fun, you also want to include some faith sharing. So at some point, invite couples to share one way in which they have seen God's Spirit active in their marriage. End the event with a blessing over the couples. This should be a significant blessing that includes a laying on of hands. Consider using the "Blessing for Those in Love" in chapter 10.

Another way to stay connected to newlyweds is to take advantage of social media. There are lots of ways to do this, and we're not going to be able to go in-depth on all of them in this book. But a simple internet search on some of the following ideas will get you started.

Text messaging: Send weekly texts to all the newlyweds in your parish that include short spiritual encouragements.

E-mail: There are lots of ways to use e-mail. For example, you can set up a series of auto-responders through a program like iContact or Constant Contact. You prewrite a weekly or monthly series of e-mails and load them into the program. Then you enter the e-mail addresses you would like the series of e-mails to be sent to. The program will send out your e-mails on the schedule you have set. Another way to use e-mail is to send a congratulations message to each couple on their one-year anniversary. You can schedule this in your auto-responder program or just put it on a physical calendar and remember to send the announcements on the right days. (You can also delegate this as a ministry to one of your newlywed couples!) Or an even simpler way is to use an online e-card service. Many services allow you to schedule e-cards to be sent whenever and to whomever you want. (You will want to be careful if a couple is struggling and you have set these messages to be sent automatically on their anniversary.)

Handwritten notes: Yes, it's old-school, but you'd be surprised how many young people today cherish receiving a handwritten note in their "snail mail" box. According to the Radicati Group, a technology market research firm, in 2012, 144 billion e-mails were sent and received worldwide. Of all the e-mail messages a person receives each day, 61 percent of that is considered nonessential.[1] A handwritten note from you will be remembered and will stand out as a genuine show of kindness.

Facebook: In Facebook, you can set up a group that is devoted exclusively to newlyweds from your parish. If you do this, make sure you have volunteers who will facilitate discussion. The newlyweds themselves are not likely to contribute much, but they will check in to see what's going on in the group. Make sure there is always something going on. Post pictures of recent weddings. Post easy-to-make dinner recipes. Post simple calls to action such as "Click 'like' if you agree with this statement from Pope Francis: 'Our prayer cannot be reduced to an hour on Sundays. It is important to have a daily relationship with the Lord.'" (You can get great pope content from his Twitter page: twitter.com/Pontifex.)

Pinterest: Pinterest is one of the fastest growing social networks out there. It is likely that many of your newlywed couples are on it—especially the women. It is a great place to post wedding photos, parish event photos, an image of your Sunday bulletin, pictures of parish staff members—especially those who newlyweds would most likely need to interact with—pictures of easy-to-make dishes, and pictures of inexpensive romantic getaways in your area. Also create a prayer board or a spirituality board, and post inspirational images with a brief prayer.

YouTube: YouTube accounts for about 28 percent of all searches on Google. Most laptops and smart phones and tablets come equipped with everything you need to make a short video. Consider posting weekly tips for your newlyweds. Tips can include prayer ideas, communication techniques, how to handle money issues, new baby issues, and ways to keep the romance alive.

Parish involvement: If you spent significant time getting to know the newlyweds during the preparation process, you already know what their skills and interests are. Invite them into one of your parish ministries based on what you know about them. The invitation needs to be personal. Face-to-face is best. A phone call is second best. E-mail won't generate much response, and a general announcement will generate zero response.

"Oldly" weds: Consider scheduling an anniversary party for the long-time married couples in your parish. Single out those with twenty-five- and fifty-year (or whatever) milestones for special recognition. This is great for the older couples in the parish. But the main reason to do it is to invite the newlyweds to serve as volunteers to facilitate the event. It gives the newlyweds an easy way to participate in the parish, and it identifies for them who the role models are that they can emulate. (Be sure to get lots of pictures for your social media outlets!) And use the new and beautiful option for renewing vows found in the Order of Celebrating Marriage.

Sponsor couples: We talked about sponsor couples in chapter 6. You might ask the same sponsor couples to schedule four to six double dates with their newlywed couple during their first year of marriage. Or ask a new sponsor couple to step in and take on this ministry.

New baby night: Schedule an evening once or twice a year to discuss new baby issues. Be sure to include information about your baptismal preparation process. Design the night so that those who already have new babies can bring them along, and have babysitters on hand to assist new parents during the gathering. (Don't forget to take pictures!)

Retreat weekend: Schedule a day or a couple days for an annual retreat for newlyweds.

Domestic Church

It is also important during the newlyweds' first year to help them set up their domestic church. Ideally, you would have started planting these seeds during their preparation process.

"Domestic church" is not a quaint expression, and it is not meant to be reduced to "prayer at home." The Second Vatican Council said that the family, as a domestic church, exercises the priesthood of the baptized in a privileged way. We do this by living the way of faith that we spoke of earlier. In particular, we exercise our priesthood by

- celebrating the sacraments;
- offering prayer and thanksgiving;
- giving witness to a life of holiness;
- denying ourselves for the sake of others;
- giving generously to those in need (see *Catechism of the Catholic Church*, 167).

It is important that in the newlyweds' first year of marriage, parishes help them understand and live the difference between *going* to church and *being* church.

We realize that many newlywed couples are barely catechized, and trying to help them understand their role in the priesthood of the baptized is a challenge. But it is not a challenge that is beyond us. If your preparation process was truly conversion centered, as we have been urging, then the effects of that conversion will have begun to take root in the newlyweds. The task before you now is to nurture that conversion and bring it to fruition.

As you know, the couples who come to us are usually not completely irreligious. Most have an initial level of faith and more than a few have quite a deep faith. What they often lack is the discipline of a Christian lifestyle to strengthen that faith.

Now, we do not recommend you rush right out and tell your newlyweds that they have to begin living a disciplined Christian lifestyle. That will have about as much success as telling a three-year-old he has to eat his lima beans.

But what if you say something like this? What if you ask newlyweds what their hopes are for their new family? Would they like their home to be a place of tenderness? a place where second chances and forgiveness are the norm? a place where everyone who lives there respects and honors everyone else who lives there? Would they like their home to be built on rock-solid faithfulness to one another? Would they like their home to be a place where they do favors for each other—wild, crazy, generous favors—without anyone keeping score of who did what for whom?

These are exactly the values of disciplined life listed in the *Catechism of the Catholic Church* (see 2223). We think this is exactly the kind of home most newlyweds long for. But you can't build a home like this on wishes. It takes training, endurance, patience, mistake-making, getting-back-upness, tears, laughter, and just plain grit. Most of all it takes prayer and knowing that without God's help, we don't have much of a chance.

This is where you come in. You can provide the training and support newlyweds need to *be* church. Before we look at how to do that, however, we need to chat. Those of us who have worked in parish staffs, and even those who never have but have served as dedicated volunteers—well, we don't think straight all the time. We spend so much creative energy building amazing, creative programs at the parish that we lose sight of the fact that the parish is not the main arena of spiritual life. Just because we spend most of our waking moments on the parish campus does not mean that other people should. In fact, the bulk of prayer and faith building happens in the homes in our neighborhoods—not at church. We have to remember that and integrate that knowledge deep into our creative spots so we don't lose focus. Building programs at church is a good thing, but it is a secondary thing. The primary thing is training Christian families how to be church—domestic church—right in their own homes.

Bill Huebsch, a nationally known catechist and writer, identifies several steps for building up households of faith.[2] For the newlyweds of the parish, we're going to focus on two of his steps:

- 50-50 agreements
- Formal listening sessions

50-50 Agreements

There are two key components to 50-50 agreements. First, parish leaders have to recognize that many, many elements of a Christian lifestyle are already taking place in parishioners' homes—even the homes of barely catechized newlyweds. Establishing a Christian lifestyle is often not our first task. Our first task is to recognize and affirm the Christian activity that is already taking place.

The second component is to make these Christian behaviors explicit and reinforce them. Here are just a few things taking place in the homes of your newlyweds that give witness to a Christian life:

- Hugging
- Kissing
- Forgiving
- Healing
- Recycling
- Worrying
- Praying
- Nursing
- Sharing
- Surprising
- Feeding
- Donating
- Dining
- Gifting
- Loving

Huebsch suggests we ask households to write down all the things they do for each other that go into building up the family. We then might suggest some additional things that might have been left off the list (for example, regular participation in Sunday liturgy). These behaviors would be written in the form of promises the family makes to each other and to the parish. For example, we promise to hug each other three times a day. We promise to be responsible about recycling. We promise to pray together both at home and at Sunday Mass. Promises like these are the first 50 percent of the agreement.

The other 50 percent is promises we, as a parish, make to support the newlyweds in building their household of faith. Huebsch suggests some of the following as examples:

- Dynamic Sunday liturgy
- Meaningful (not boring) instruction in the faith
- Opportunities for sharing faith
- Ideas for marking the liturgical seasons at home
- Unconditional welcome, always, no matter what
- A rapid response to calls for help when you are sick or in trouble

The idea is that you would write this out as an actual agreement between two parties—a contract of faith—and both you and the couple would sign it. The goal, however, isn't to create a legal document. It is to make explicit the behaviors and goals of the newlyweds and the support that the parish can offer to help them with their goals. By putting these in contractual form, the couple has the opportunity to think more deeply about *how* they want to be a couple and how the parish can help.

Formal Listening Sessions

Huebsch suggests that parish council members take on the ministry of listening and offer it to the entire parish. If your parish is ready to gear up for that, you can easily schedule times when the council members can meet with the newlyweds.

However, even if you cannot yet get the parish council on board with a broad, all-parish listening process, you can still implement it on a smaller scale, focused only on the newlyweds. The basic process is that two members of the wedding preparation team (or parish council members, if they are up for it) invite the newlyweds over for dinner. At the dinner, your only agenda is to listen—to how the couple are building their household of faith, what their struggles are, what their successes and joys are, what they need more or less of from the parish. Throughout the evening, the newlyweds should do 70 percent or more of the talking.

It is important for the couple to know that you'd like to share their stories with other parish leaders. So they need to understand the boundaries of what they would like to share. And then, please do share their stories. Make sure your marriage preparation team and other parish leaders are filled in about how the newlyweds in the parish are doing with their attempts to build households of faith.

Beyond the First Year

No matter how much we work at transforming our marriage preparation processes and build up structures that support newlyweds in their first year of marriage, we can never completely protect them from the myriad challenges they will face that will test their relationship. What we *can* do, however, is keep our end of our promise to them by being present in their lives as much as we are able and by reminding them always of the unending love of Christ for them.

We can do this by first praying for them always, in our own daily prayers and in the intercessions we offer each Sunday as a community.

Second, we can continue to make Sunday at the parish something they want to be part of and ensure that the community we showed them we are during their engagement is indeed the community that will be faithful to them for life, no matter what.

Third, we do everything we can to connect and deepen the relationship that was established with them in their engagement: notes and cards on significant days, phone calls to let them know they are missed, invitations to participate more intentionally in the work of the community and the mission of Christ, blessings on their anniversaries, and open arms every time they ask for help.

And, God forbid, if the worst does happen and their marriage breaks up, we promise to stand by them both. One of the greatest burdens people feel after the marriage they have been in falls apart is the overwhelming sense that "everyone knows" and "everyone judges them," whether or not anyone says anything to them explicitly. More often than not, their community of friends and acquaintances say nothing, whether out of their own embarrassment or fear of embarrassing the couple. The worst thing we can do is isolate those who have ended a marriage, especially one we helped them prepare for.

All the care we showed and promised them in their engagement and initial year of marriage needs to be profoundly present if that marriage ends. Here, the sponsor couples can be very helpful in being a kind of "first responder" of our field-hospital church, as Pope Francis calls us to be. If they have been keeping in touch with the newlyweds throughout the first several years of their marriage, they will know when things are starting to go wrong and when more support is needed from the community of disciples.

Even if we cannot help them mend the relationship, we can still offer a welcome place to be at home and the opportunity for reconciliation in whatever way will help them keep faith and hope in God through their darkest hours.

Shortly after the 1974 provisional English translation of the RCIA appeared, Aidan Kavanagh, OSB, wrote a brief report on the state of Christian initiation in which he said,

> One may turn an altar around and leave *reform* at that. But one cannot set an adult catechumenate in motion without becoming necessarily involved with *renewal* in the ways a local church lives its faith from top to bottom. For members of an adult catechumenate must be secured through evangelization; they must be formed to maturity in ecclesial faith through catechesis both prior to baptism and after it; and there must be something to initiate them into that will be correlative to the expectations built up in them throughout their whole initiatory process. This last means a community of lively faith in Jesus Christ dead, risen, and present actually among his People. In this area, when one change occurs, all changes.[3]

In a similar way, this vision of marriage preparation based on the dynamics of the catechumenate must transform the entire parish into the community of disciples we want to be. This preparation process cannot result in only the marriage of two people. It certainly must bring about an entirely different kind of community, one that keeps its promises to all those who seek to encounter the ever-faithful Lord.

9

Three Steps to Know If a Couple Is Ready for Marriage

*M*uch of the marriage preparation literature that you'll find focuses on the psychological readiness of couples to marry. Are they mature enough? Have they discussed the important issues that will arise in their marriage? Are they compatible?

Please find a good preparation resource in this genre and use it in your process. But don't stop there. The bedrock of a Christian marriage is not psychological readiness. It is sacramental readiness. To understand what this means, let's turn again to the Rite of Christian Initiation of Adults.

New RCIA team members are often shocked to discover that part of their responsibility is to help discern the readiness of a catechumen for initiation. They wonder why they can't just leave that up to the catechumen and the Holy Spirit to decide. The confusion on the part of new RCIA team members arises because they are confusing acceptance with ability. They believe that if they discern that a catechumen is not ready for initiation, they are somehow taking over God's role, and passing judgment about the catechumen's worthiness.

If the initiation process were simply a way of determining who God loves, the new team members would be correct. But it's not. God loves the greatest sinner and the most obvious pagan just as much as God loves St. Francis and Mother Teresa. No one has to get baptized in order to receive God's love. That is not what RCIA teams are discerning.

The RCIA is an apprenticeship process that trains catechumens in how to live a Christian life. And, as we said before, that life is a journey to the cross. It is a constant dying to ourselves. To do that, you need skills. The initiation process is about training catechumens in those skills so that they will be able to live up to their baptismal promises. And the RCIA is very clear about what those skills are. So discernment is not some mysterious revelation that happens in secret consultation with an unseen God. It is a very straightforward, upfront, clear look at each catechumen's skill level. When a catechumen has reached a minimum level of skill as defined in the RCIA, he or she is ready for initiation.

It should be that way with weddings also. In fact, it is that way when we focus on psychological readiness. We do all kinds of things to couples to make sure they have the psychological skills they need for marriage. But often, we skip over the skills of discipleship they will need for the Christian vocation of marriage.

So where do we find the skills of discipleship needed for Christian marriage? Where do we find the list of skills couples will need in order to make their marriage a sacramental journey? We are going to look in three places: the Order of Celebrating Marriage, Scripture, and the teaching of the church.

Order of Celebrating Marriage

The actual marriage rite begins immediately after the homily. The presider invites the wedding couple and their witnesses to stand. He then says the following:

> Dearly beloved,
> you have come together into the house of the Church,
> so that in the presence of the Church's minister and the community
> your intention to commit yourselves to Marriage
> may be strengthened by the Lord with a sacred seal.
> Christ abundantly blesses the love that binds you.
> Through a special Sacrament,
> he enriches and strengthens
> those he has already consecrated by Holy Baptism,
> that they may be faithful to each other for ever
> and assume all the responsibilities of married life.

And so, in the presence of the Church,
I ask you to state your intentions. (OCM, 59)

The purpose of the introduction is to remind everyone that this sacrament, like all sacraments, is rooted in baptism. The introductory comments also remind everyone that a sacrament is an event of Jesus Christ.

First Skill Level

As we prepare couples for their celebration of marriage, we need to discern their readiness for the sacrament at this basic, baptismal level. Assuming they are both baptized, does the couple recognize that their marriage is an extension of their baptismal discipleship? Do they understand, at least at a basic level, that their marriage is an event of Jesus Christ?

This might be difficult to discern. For many couples, marriage in a church is a cultural event more than an event of discipleship. But we can't be too hasty in that judgment. Beneath a couple's cultural reflexes, there may be a level of faith that is not at first very evident. We can find some help in our discernment in the RCIA. For those who are beginners in faith, the RCIA asks that their catechists look for these behaviors as readiness for celebrating the sacraments:

- Shown a conversion in mind and action
- Shown a sufficient acquaintance with Christian teaching
- Shown a spirit of faith and charity (see RCIA, 120)

If you can say that your couples have shown these behaviors, you can be confident they have reached the first skill level of readiness.

Unbaptized Candidates

If one or both members of the couple are unbaptized, you would use a different form of the marriage rite, and the presider would not refer to the consecration of baptism (see Order of Celebrating Marriage, 158). However, we would assume that at least one of the couple is preparing for baptism. Otherwise, why are they asking to be married in the church? We can turn again to the RCIA for criteria

for readiness of those who are at the beginning stages of their relationship with the risen Christ and apply those criteria to this stage of
readiness for Christian marriage. See RCIA 42 for the prerequisites
for becoming a catechumen.

Second Skill Level

If the couple have a living, personal relationship with Christ, it is
that relationship that has brought them to this place on their journey. They will then stand before the Body of Christ—the gathered
Christian assembly—and state their intentions:

> N. and N., have you come here to enter into Marriage
> without coercion,
> freely and wholeheartedly?
>
> Are you prepared, as you follow the path of Marriage,
> to love and honor each other
> for as long as you both shall live?
>
> Are you prepared to accept children lovingly from God
> and to bring them up
> according to the law of Christ and his Church? (OCM, 60)

Our preparation process must, of course, give couples the skills they
will need to be able to answer yes to these questions. (The final
question is omitted for couples who are not able to have children.)

See chapter 2 for some ideas on how to use these questions to
discern readiness throughout the marriage preparation process.

Third Skill Level

In the movies, the big climax is the moment when the minister says,
"You may now kiss the bride." But in the Catholic rite, the promise
is the high point. Everything in the rite leads to and flows from the
consent or the promise. The bride and groom each make, essentially,
two promises to each other:

1. To be faithful to the other, no matter what
2. To love and honor the other forever (see OCM, 62)

We don't have to tell you, this is huge. These seem like almost impossible promises to make. Nevertheless, our processes must help the couples recognize both the enormity of these promises and the even more enormous power of God's love to help us keep them. We see this stage of readiness as similar to the period of purification and enlightenment in the initiation process. Once it dawns on the catechumen how *big* his or her baptism is going to be, spiritual warfare breaks out. The catechumen may be tempted to step back, to not take the plunge. In this final preparation period, the church prays fervently that any darkness that might remain in the catechumen be finally vanquished. And the church prays that all the gifts and strengths that God has graced the catechumen with will grow more powerful and strong.

As we said in chapter 7, we would like to see a similar period in the marriage preparation process during which the church and the couple together enter into a time of spiritual retreat. During that time, we would pray that God's Spirit would "purify the minds and hearts" of the couple and that they would be enlightened "with a deeper knowledge of Christ the Savior" (see RCIA, 139).

If we could imagine a parallel final preparation for the engaged couple, it might not be as fully intense as Lent is for the catechumens and the parish. But it might include Lenten elements that help strengthen them spiritually. So, for example, the couple might be asked to enter into a time of more intense prayer. We might ask them to search their hearts and minds more diligently for any final traces of hesitation or fear. We might pray blessings over them more frequently, perhaps even daily. We might even ask them to fast for a day or two before their wedding. Not a total fast. We don't want anyone fainting at the altar. But how many brides (and perhaps grooms) diet before the wedding so as to fit more easily into their wedding garments? Perhaps we could put a more spiritual spin on their abstinence from food.

Scripture

The Bible is the inspired word of God. Even so, it is not the "last word." The *Catechism of the Catholic Church* says, "The Christian faith is not a 'religion of the book'" (108). That means that Jesus Christ is the living Word, and we must always interpret the words of Scripture through our relationship with the risen Christ. The skill that engaged couples must master is the ability to hear and read Scripture in a way that makes them attentive to how God is calling them to holiness at this very moment in their lives.

The attentiveness to God's call is especially important when choosing Scriptures for their wedding. With the post–Vatican II revision of the rite, wedding couples now have dozens of readings to choose from. This rich selection of choices is a reminder that sacraments always flow from God's word. The homily, which will be based on the couple's selection of readings, speaks about the mystery of Christian marriage, the dignity of married love, the grace of the sacrament, and the responsibilities of married people, keeping in mind the circumstances of the particular couple being married (see OCM, 57).

Oftentimes, the couple will leave the selection of readings up to the presider. This is unfortunate. Drawing on the catechumenate as a model, one of the key factors in the preparation of the engaged couple will be an acquaintance with the teachings of the church as they flow from the word of God (see RCIA, 75.1). Their level of engagement with the Scriptures, especially their concern for those that will be proclaimed at their wedding, will also be a marker of their readiness to enter into a sacramental marriage.

In chapter 4, we discussed how to use the Sunday and weekday readings as a springboard for catechesis. In addition, the wedding rite has its own set of readings that can lead to deeper reflection on how God is calling each particular couple to live out their discipleship. Indeed, the readings selected for the celebration of marriage will have "a great impact in the handing on of catechesis about the Sacrament itself and about the duties of the spouses" (OCM, 34).

Instead of allowing the couple to default to the presider's choice of readings, consider incorporating faith sharing and catechetical reflection on the possible readings for the marriage rite into your preparation process. Use the techniques discussed in chapter 4 along with the following reading options to teach some of these key aspects of Catholic faith.

- Genesis 1:26-28, 31a—We are made in God's image
- Genesis 2:18-24—The unity of man and woman is part of God's plan from the beginning

- Song of Songs 2:8-10, 14, 16a; 8:6-7a—Love is holy; it is the fundamental vocation of every person
- Ephesians 5:2a, 25-32—We are called to sacrifice for one another
- Romans 8:31b-35, 37-39—Christ is the source of the grace of married love and commitment
- 1 John 3:18-24—The way of marriage gives witness to the way of Christ
- Matthew 19:3-6—The bond of marriage is eternal
- Mark 10:6-9—God is the author of marriage; the vocation to marriage is part of human nature
- John 2:1-11—Marriage is a sign of the new covenant and of the heavenly banquet

Teaching of the Church

At the Second Vatican Council, the church went to great lengths to emphasize our call to holiness. Previous to the council, some thought that holiness was reserved to a special few. But the teaching of the council reminds us that all of God's creation is filled with the holiness of God. In particular, marriage is one of the central ways in which Christians realize their holiness:

> In virtue of the sacrament of Matrimony by which they signify and share in (see Eph 5:32) the mystery of the unity and fruitful love between Christ and the church, christian married couples help one another to attain holiness in their married life and in accepting and educating their children. (Dogmatic Constitution on the Church, 11)

So here is a skill that you want to look for in a couple before they get married because this skill is needed for a sacramental marriage. Spouses have to "signify and share in . . . the mystery of . . . Christ." Okay, let's break that apart a little, because that doesn't sound much like a skill.

"Signify" is a churchy term that means show or say something important and meaningful. In baptism, when we immerse someone in water and say, "I baptize you in the name of the Father, and of the Son, and of the Holy Spirit," it has meaning. It means this person is now part of God's family, part of the Body of Christ. It's real, and it's important.

When a married couple "signify" the mystery of Christ, they are showing, through their marriage, that all Christians are "married" to Christ, just as this husband and wife are married to each other. The Catechism says,

> The entire Christian life bears the mark of the spousal love of Christ and the Church. Already Baptism, the entry into the People of God, is a nuptial mystery; it is so to speak the nuptial bath [cf. Eph 5:26-27] which precedes the wedding feast, the Eucharist. Christian marriage in its turn becomes an efficacious sign, the sacrament of the covenant of Christ and the Church. Since it *signifies* and communicates grace, marriage between baptized persons is a true sacrament of the New Covenant [cf. DS 1800; CIC, can. 1055 § 2]. (1617, emphasis added)

The task before you is to ask, How is our marriage preparation process training couples to be an effective sign of Christ's spouse-like love for each of his people? For each couple, you need to discern if they have that skill and if they are ready to use it.

The doing of this skill—being an effective sign of Christ's spouse-like love—relates directly to holiness. Holiness isn't just about being spiritual or pious. To be holy is to be chosen for some important task. Our task, what we are chosen for, is to follow the way of Christ—a path that always leads to the cross.

The skill that spouses need is the ability to help each other follow Christ and thereby "attain holiness." In the day-to-day of married life and raising children, this means helping each other learn to die to oneself. And we do this first of all by example. I (Nick) help my spouse learn to sacrifice her ego and her needs by first of all sacrificing my own. Does our marriage preparation process teach this skill, and do we have a way to measure if the skill has been learned?

A Three-Step Discernment Process

Sometimes we think of "God's will" as an inscrutable puzzle that only wizened old monks who have meditated for decades in caves or on mountaintops can discern.

But that simply isn't so. God wants us to know God's will. Saint Paul tells us that "he has made known to us the mystery of his will" (Eph 1:9).

So when it comes to discernment of sacramental readiness for marriage, we cannot just throw up our hands as though it is impossible to know the whims of a fleeting Holy Spirit. God is giving us clear, unmistakable signs. Our job is to understand them and act upon them.

A true discernment process does not start with the engaged couple. It starts with us. According to Timothy M. Gallagher, OMV, in *The Discernment of Spirits*, a discernment process has three movements:

- Be aware
- Understand
- Take action

Be Aware

The first movement is that we have to be aware of what is going on. It is somewhat easy to understand what is going on outside of us. The harder challenge is to become aware of what is going on inside of us. In fact, we can sometimes focus on external activity as a way of distracting ourselves from paying attention to our interior thoughts and feelings.

Gallagher says it takes real courage to focus on our spiritual awareness. He says spiritual awareness is the fundamental first step to all other aspects of discernment.

We can't do any real discernment until we are aware of our own spiritual interior. So this initial movement—being aware—needs some serious attention from us.

Understand

The second step is to understand where the Spirit is leading us and leading the engaged couple. When we quiet ourselves and think about a particular engaged person, does our spiritual awareness of that person bear the signs of God? Are we happy and peaceful when we think about how that person has met or tried to meet the objective criteria laid out in the Order of Celebrating Marriage, the Scriptures, and the teaching of the church? Do we feel a sense of joy when we imagine the person trying to live a life based on the skills they will need for a sacramental marriage?

On the other hand, even if the couple has objectively met all the criteria asked, do we feel dejected and a little sad about them? Do we get anxious when we think about celebrating marriage with this couple?

This second step, understanding, is critically important. It is much more than a simple list of things a couple needs to cross off their to-do list. It is a deep, spiritual understanding of the will of God. We have to take the time to first pay attention to and then understand where God is leading us and the couple.

For each couple, you might ask yourselves questions such as these:

- Imagine your couple a year from now. Do you have a strong hope they will have grown more deeply in their faith? From what you know of them right now, do you feel joyful about the possibilities before them?

- Contemplate the next significant step before your couple. Imagine they take that step. How does that make you feel? Imagine they do not take that step at this time. How does *that* make you feel? The outcome that gives you more peace is more likely of God.

- Knowing God's will is often easy. Carrying it out is sometimes difficult. Are you feeling any anxiety or discomfort about your couple? Where is that discomfort coming from? Is it because you might have to be the bearer of difficult news? Or is there something about the couple that makes you uncomfortable? If you could remove any potential interpersonal conflict and move directly to a solution, what would that look like?

- As you pray about your couple, are you the only one on your team that is experiencing joy (or discomfort)? If so, what might God be saying to you? Is your own spirit being drawn toward God or away from God?

Take Action

The final step in the discernment process is to take action. We can't really say we have done discernment unless we act on what we have discovered in the process. There are two possible actions to take.

The first is to reject the path you had been considering. If you discerned that God is not leading you to that path, set it aside. Don't fret over it, and don't return to it. Take the action, and move forward.

The second possible action is to accept that God is calling you to this path. In that case, go for it! And don't do it halfheartedly. If this path is truly God's call, you should do everything you can to follow the Spirit's urging. If the path becomes difficult ahead, stay faithful and stay confident.

Are We Being Too Judgmental?

One thing that gets in the way of a good discernment process is our own fears about being judgmental. We don't want to be in the position of telling a couple they are not ready for marriage. We don't want to be responsible for holding them back. For those of us who think that way, we need to change our mindset. Think of yourself as a skydiving instructor. If you push novice skydivers out the door of the airplane before they're ready—or allow them to jump on their own when you know they're not ready—you are putting them at great risk.

The same is true with marriage. If we ask couples to follow the way of marriage—to live a life of sacrifice modeled on Christ—before they are ready, the risk that they will fall away from their commitment is great.

You may not be able to dissuade a couple you discern not to be ready from getting married, but that shouldn't stop you from sharing your concerns. Also, your concerns should not come out of the blue, as though you went to the mountaintop to receive God's personal word to you, and now you've descended to deliver it.

Discernment should be an ongoing process with you and the couple throughout the entire preparation process. If you have spent some time deeply listening to the couple, you will know what their own goals are for their marriage.

Together, you and the couple will work to align those goals with the sacramental skills for marriage we discussed above. We suggest even writing that down, so you and the couple know what skills they are working toward in the preparation process. (See "Preparing a Personalized Formation Plan for Each Couple" in chapter 5.)

And then, on a regular basis (perhaps weekly), you and the couple will discern together how well they are doing on building their skills. A regular, ongoing discernment process is a healthy collaboration between you and the couple that will enable them to be as prepared as possible for their marriage.

10

Rituals for Marking Stages

The official text of the Order of Celebrating Marriage includes not only the prayers for the wedding rite itself and all its various forms but also blessings for the engaged couple and for a married couple on their anniversary. These are official rites of the church. However, prayer and blessings are not limited to these discrete moments alone. The entire life of a couple should be marked at significant moments by prayer, ritual, and blessing.

This chapter includes suggestions for prayers, rituals, and blessings. Some are formal and official rites; most are informal and everyday rites for remembering God's presence in our daily lives.

A Note about Blessings and Other Sacramentals

> Finally, all of you, be of one mind, sympathetic, loving toward one another, compassionate, humble. Do not return evil for evil, or insult for insult; but, on the contrary, a blessing, because to this you were called, that you might inherit a blessing. (1 Pet 3:8-9)

Blessings are part of an entire family of Christian disciplines called sacramentals. These include making the sign of the cross on yourself or another person, signing yourself with holy water, receiving ashes on your forehead, or blessing things, like meals, cars, homes, or other people. Sacramentals are outward signs and actions that remind us of the grace we have received in a sacrament. These small-s sacramentals, thus, flow from and lead us back to celebrating the big-S sacraments and help to shape our daily attitudes to reflect the grace given in the sacraments we celebrate.

Sign of the Cross

A very simple sacramental to start with is the sign of the cross. Ask couples to commit to making the sign of the cross on themselves on a daily basis—perhaps when they wake or before they go to bed, or as they leave for work. This sign reminds them that they belong to Christ whose daily mission on earth was to love others and to show God's love for them. Ask them to be attentive to blessing themselves with holy water every time they enter and leave the church. This reminds them of their baptism and their unique call to be members of Christ's Body, the church.

If one of the couple is not baptized, he or she can still make the sign of the cross, but the meaning of the actions would be different. Making the sign of the cross might be a sign of support for the baptized fiancé(e) and the faith he or she professes. Or it might show a desire to learn more about the Christian way of life and to become baptized. Whatever their reasons may be, sharing in the sign of the cross can help strengthen the bond between the partners and their bond to the Christian community.

Blessings

There are three important things to understand about blessings. First, they are not some kind of "magic spell" or incantation that guarantees protection or good fortune, as if we can just call upon God to do something, and God will do it. God doesn't work that way. God is a blesser. From the beginning of creation, God blesses. That's just what God does. God is constantly giving and communicating himself to his creatures. God desires and longs to be in relationship with us and, therefore, blesses us. Our response to God's blessing—God's grace—is to praise God, which itself is a blessing of God. God's blessings and our blessings of God is a continual dialogue that deepens the bond established from the beginning between God and all creation.

The second thing to remember about blessings is that we need to be good stewards of what has been given to us if we want to genuinely praise God for God's graces to us. Therefore we ask God to bless the things we use so that we might use them to extend God's blessing to others. We ask God to bless the people we love so that they might be strengthened, in turn, to bless and praise God. Thus, blessings are a kind of social contract. It's a recognition of God's gift and a petition asking God that we might use his gifts well for the good of others.

The third thing to understand about blessings is that they remind us that we depend on God. In other words, we can't do it alone. God is always the one who helps us in our time of need, who strengthens us to do what we are called to, and who enables us to be who God needs us to be for the world. Blessings keep us humble and strengthen our love for God.

The Four-Part Blessing Structure

Almost all blessings have the same structure. Once you learn this easy four-part structure, you can write your own blessings too!

1. We Name God

In the first part, we name God. Sometimes it's as simple as "Lord God" or "Father," or it can be a longer title, such as "God, Creator of heaven and earth."

2. We Recall What God Has Done

The second part reminds us of what God has done for us in the past. A blessing for a home might recall how God has been a home for those who wander or are lost. Often, you'll hear references to passages in the Bible or stories of how God did something good for our ancestors in faith.

3. We Ask God to Do It Again

Just as God has been good to us in the past, we ask God to do something good again for this particular person or in this particular situation.

4. We Ask in the Name of Jesus

The last part of the blessing recalls that it is Christ in whose name we pray. So a common ending for blessings is "We ask this through Christ our Lord. Amen."

A simple way to remember this blessing structure is to think of You-Who-Do-Through.

- You: name God
- Who: remember what God has done in the past
- Do: ask God to do that good thing again now
- Through: ask it through Christ

As you look through the blessings in this chapter, see if you can spot this four-part structure. And encourage your couples to experiment and write their own blessings. As they practice by writing down some blessings, they will get better and more comfortable with the structure that they will be able to improvise their own prayers on the spot. These can be very useful for occasions such as mealtime prayers at home and the many times during their preparation when they will gather with friends and family around a meal.

A Note on Ritual Books

The Order of Celebrating Marriage and the *Book of Blessings* are universal ritual books of the church, meaning that they are official texts that are used around the world, translated into the various languages of the church, and adapted and approved for use by each country's conference of bishops. These books are typically found in parish sacristies, and most pastors and other pastoral leaders might have their own copies. Although the prayers and blessings found in these books pertain to many of the situations encountered by engaged and married couples, they would not necessarily need a copy of the books themselves since they are primarily for the use of pastors and other parish leaders.

The *Catholic Household Blessings and Prayers*, however, is certainly a book that can be given to an engaged couple for their personal use as individuals and in their home together. This is a local ritual book, meaning that it was prepared by a country's local conference of bishops for use within that country. In the United States, our conference is called the United States Conference of Catholic Bishops (USCCB). They prepared this ritual book, taking some of the official rites from the universal books that could be led by a layperson and adding other prayers and blessings that baptized persons can use for themselves or for others in their household. In addition, there are prayers that parents can teach their children and Scripture texts listed by theme in order to encourage us in particular times of distress, anxiety, or joy. This book is meant to be shared, given, and used by every Catholic family. It would be a very appropriate gift for the parish or the sponsor couple to give to each couple as they enter the final stage of their preparation for marriage. (This book is available from the USCCB publishing department: usccbpublishing.org.)

Blessings and Prayers before the Engagement

A Prayer for Help Deciding Whether or Not to Propose

Thank you, God, for the gift of this relationship with your
daughter/son, N.
I have learned so much about myself and about what it
means to love,
and I desire so much to share myself and that love with
her/him even more.
Grant me wisdom in this time of discernment
to know if the time is right
to make a decision about the rest of our lives.
Give us both patience to trust in your timing
and clarity to see the choices we must make.
Help us persevere in love on this journey,
but also teach us to gently let go
if you call us to different paths.
And if your will for us is a lifetime together,
fill me with your love and peace
that I may be ever humble in my asking
and hopeful in her/his response.
Amen.

Before Meeting Your Partner's Parents for the First Time

Lord, you know everything about me,
all my thoughts, hopes, and dreams,
my disappointments and regrets,
and all the good and not-so-good things about who I am.

As I meet N.'s parents for the first time,
please help me make a good impression on them.
Let them see my best self, the way N. sees me.
Most of all, let them know how much I love their son/
    daughter,
all my hopes and dreams for our life together,
and how much I would give to make him/her happy forever.
As I begin this relationship with N.'s family,
let us be gentle with one another
as we grow to know each other more and more
and, in time, come to love one another as one family.

Amen.

Blessings and Prayers for the Engagement

During the catechumenate period in the Rite of Christian Initiation of Adults, catechumens participate in special blessings and prayers that serve not only to increase their faith and support their apprenticeship in the Christian life but also to mark their passage from one level of formation to another.

For those preparing for marriage, the engagement period may be seen as a similar period during which the engaged couples participate in special blessings and prayers that deepen their preparation, remove any lingering doubts, purify intentions, and mark their progression toward marriage. Note that in the RCIA, the prayers and blessings during this period vary in their language and intention in order to reflect the growth that one sees in the catechumen through the course of this period. This progressive and gradual nature of preparation also should be reflected in the kinds of prayers and blessings we might celebrate with the engaged couple. Therefore, pay attention to the specific needs of each couple at that particular time of their engagement, and select an appropriate prayer text or blessing that reflects where they are in that stage of preparation.

Pedir la Mano

In the Hispanic tradition, the participation of the families is very important in the entire act of the proposal and engagement. The custom called *pedir la mano* ("asking for the hand") is a traditional way of involving the families and the parish communities of the couple. (In this ritual, it is assumed that the man is the one making the proposal. However, today, that is not always the case. Yet the principle of involving the entire family can still be followed in this ritual, regardless of who does the asking.)

The first part of the tradition calls for the family of the one proposing to meet with the family of the one being proposed to in order to ask for permission for the potential marriage to happen. If the receiving family agrees, then the person proposing makes the actual proposal right there in front of everyone, including the family's parish priest! Assuming the answer to the proposal is positive, then, at the end of a Sunday Mass, the newly engaged couple receives a blessing from their parents and from the parish community.

Gathering both parties' families might seem like an intrusion into this very personal moment. But lately, at least on the internet, there's been a trend of coordinating very public proposals—often including flash-mob-style music and choreography—that involve both parties' families and friends and are witnessed by any passersby who happen upon the moment. In a small way, some of the meaning of *pedir la mano* has perhaps caught on in popular culture. Marriage is more than just the joining of two people. It joins family to family and is strengthened and supported by that wider union. Especially when children from previous relationships are involved, inviting each person's family into the proposal event and asking for their support in this next important step of the relationship provides the encouragement and network of help the couple will need to sustain their marriage.

There are no specific prayers or rituals that accompany the *pedir la mano*, but here are some prayers that can be used by the couple and their families during the time of the proposal.

A Parent's Blessing of One's Son or Daughter before the Proposal

Lord God, you gave me the gift of my son/daughter, N.,
and I have watched him/her grow more beautiful with
    each passing day.
I know he/she is precious in your eyes, as he/she is in mine,
and now another person recognizes that too.
Be with them both in this time of excitement, nervousness,
    and discernment.

Help them enter into this new part of their relationship
  with hope
and with reverence for the decisions they will make.
Let the disappointments that may come not be too
  painful to bear,
and may their joys be magnified by your delight in them.
Whatever may come in the journey you have prepared
  for my child,
may he/she always trust in my love for him/her,
which is only a small reflection of your great love for us all.
Amen.

A Prayer Over an Engagement Ring before the Proposal

Lord, be with me as I prepare to ask the biggest question
  of my life.
Let this ring be a sign of my unending love
and a reflection of the treasure she/he is to me.
May she/he accept this ring and all that it represents with
  love and hope,
and may we always have faith in your endless care for us,
encircling us with joy forever.
Amen.

"Thanksgiving upon Receiving Good News" (*from* The Work of
Your Hands,[1] *p. 25*)

Sometimes we get into the habit of praying only when we need
something or find ourselves in a difficult situation. However, we
also need to cultivate the habit of praying when things are good,
especially when wonderful things happen to us, as a reminder that
all good things come from God, the source of all goodness. Here's a
prayer family members and friends might pray when they find out
about a pending engagement and one the couple might pray after
the proposal when the answer is "yes":

Blessed are you, Lord God, who bring us good news!
When the years had worn on, barren and joyless,
you came to our door as angels in disguise,
blessing our home with new life and laughter.

When all seemed dark and despair overshadowed us,
you met us on the road as an unexpected stranger,
opening our eyes and hearts to the fire of your love.

And as we wept at the mouth of the tomb in a springtime garden,
you spoke our name, concealed as a common field hand,
sending us out to proclaim, "We have seen the Lord!"

We praise you and we bless you
for the good news you bring us this day.
Make us bearers of your life-giving message
that fills our world with wonder, hope, and surprise.
Amen.

A Blessing of Families and Friends after the Proposal

If the parish priest, deacon, or other parish minister or family friend is present at the proposal, this blessing might be used over the two families who will now become one in the union of their son and daughter:

God, our Father,
in your goodness, you have called together this man and
    woman
that they may become one in marriage.
In your love, bless now their families and all who are dear
    to them.
May N. and N. find in each of them a constant source of
    support
and true companions in times of need.
Let their families and friends grow closer to one another
    during this engagement
that they may all become a new family,
inspired by the love of husband and wife
and nourished by your divine love that gives life to all
    people.
We ask this through Christ, our Lord.
Amen.

The Order of Blessing an Engaged Couple

The church has an official ritual for blessing the engagement called "The Order of Blessing an Engaged Couple," which is found in the *Order of Celebrating Marriage*, 253–71. It is also found in the *Book of Blessings*, 195–214, and in *Catholic Household Blessings and Prayers*, part IV, 247–51. The official leader of the blessing may be one of the parents, or, if there is a priest or a deacon present, he would lead the blessing. If there is another lay minister present who holds a special significance with the family, that person might lead the blessing. It may take place in the family's home or other family or church gathering. This ritual also includes a blessing of the engagement rings.

Note that the ritual text does not allow for this official blessing to take place during a Mass (possibly because it would look too similar to a sacramental marriage rite). However, a very brief prayer might be said for the couple at the end of Mass and led by their parents in front of the parish assembly. Also note that actual wedding proposals should not take place within a Mass.

Presenting the Vows

See chapter 7, "Spiritual Preparation for the Rite," for a ritual outline for presenting the wedding vows to the couple in the months before their wedding.

Daily Prayers

Prayers of a Future Husband or Wife

In part IV of *Catholic Household Blessings and Prayers*, there are two prayers based on Scripture given for the future husband and wife to pray in their own personal prayers.

The "Prayer of a Future Husband" is based on a passage from the book of Tobit, about the story of Tobiah and Sarah, only children who overcome great loss, danger, and a family curse because of their trust in God's mercy. That trust allows them to follow divine providence, to be compassionate to others even when it is inconvenient, and to give freely of what they have even though they themselves do not have much. This prayer is based on Sarah and Tobiah's prayer on their wedding night, which is also one of the options for the Old Testament reading in the Liturgy of the Word for the Rite of Marriage.

The "Prayer of a Future Wife" comes from Psalm 16. The Psalms are a book of songs that one might call the songbook of Jesus. The texts found in the Psalms are songs of praise, thanksgiving, and lament, written to be used in liturgical rites as well as personal prayer. If you read through the 150 psalms, you will find every human emotion, all placed in the context of a relationship of trust in God. Even the psalms of lament that begin with anger toward God lead to and end with a statement of trust in God's mercy. Psalm 16 is a psalm of praise for God who protects his children and prepares a joyful path for those who follow him.

"Prayer for Good Speech" (from Work of Your Hands, *pp. 26–27)*

Trying to keep track of all the details and managing the stresses of wedding planning can make anyone short on patience. When this happens, it becomes very easy to say hurtful things we don't really mean or avoid the things we should be saying. Perhaps this might be a daily prayer during those particularly overwhelming days right before the wedding:

Gracious God, with only words
you created the universe and called it "good."
Help me, then, to use my words well,
to create only life and give blessing this day.

You numbered the stars and called each one by name.
Let me cherish each person I meet
and speak their name with reverence.

You promised that your word is very near to us,
already in our mouths and in our hearts.
Give me your Spirit, and teach me what to say.
Stand guard over my mouth and temper my heart
when emotions race and words so easily cut.
Help me know when to speak up,
to be a cry for the poor and a voice in the desert,
and teach me the wisdom to know when to be silent.

Your words calmed the seas, raised the dead,
forgave the sinner, and comforted the mourning.
Give me the grace to speak the simple words:
"Please" and "Thank you." "Yes." "I love you."
And strengthen me to say the words that need to be said:
"I was wrong." "I'm sorry." "Forgive me." "I forgive you."
Let my "yes" be "yes," my "no" mean "no,"
and my promises be kept.

Above all, may I remember that
even if I speak with the tongues of angels,
yet do not have love, I am simply making noise.
So let my tongue be silenced if ever I forget you.

Lord, today, make me your word and open my lips, (†)*
and my mouth shall proclaim your praise.

Make the sign of the cross on your lips.

A Prayer When Receiving Troubling News

Lord, today I received some terrible news,
and I can't help but feel the way Martha and Mary felt
at their brother's own tomb:
Lord, if you had been here,
if you had done something, anything,
this wouldn't have happened.
Yet, I know, Lord, that you, too, could not bear that news,
and you wept under its weight.
So forgive me for blaming you
and for thinking that you have no care for us.
Help me learn from the faith of Martha and the love of
    Mary,
and teach me to trust in the Father as you did on that day.
For in the Father's tender care,
no thought of ours is left unguarded
no tear unheeded,
and no prayer by those who believe goes unheard.
Amen.

A Blessing for a Fiancé before He Leaves on a Trip (based on "Traveler's Prayer," Work of Your Hands, *p. 40)*

Lord, I ask you to bless N. as he begins this adventure.
[Make the sign of the cross on his forehead.]
Open his eyes to see you in the people he will meet.
Open his ears to hear your word in new and surprising
  ways.
Open his hands to be your blessing in whatever situation
  he finds himself.
And open his heart to receive you wherever he may go.
Protect him from harm as he travels
and give your wisdom to those he relies on for safety.
When his travel is ended and his journey complete,
bring my love home again to me renewed by your presence.
Amen.

A Blessing for a Fiancée before She Leaves on a Trip (based on "Traveler's Prayer," Work of Your Hands, *p. 40)*

Lord, I ask you to bless N. as she begins this adventure.
[Make the sign of the cross on her forehead.]
Open her eyes to see you in the people she will meet.
Open her ears to hear your word in new and surprising ways.
Open her hands to be your blessing in whatever situation
  she finds herself.
And open her heart to receive you wherever she may go.
Protect her from harm as she travels
and give your wisdom to those she relies on for safety.
When her travel is ended and her journey complete,
bring my love home again to me renewed by your presence.
Amen.

"Prayer When Lighting Candles" (from Work of Your Hands, *p. 30)*

Whether it's a birthday candle, one on your dinner table or in your bedroom, or one lit in prayer or remembrance of a loved one, the symbol of light holds a special place in Catholic ritual. It was

God's first act of creation, and it is a significant way we talk about Christ, the Light of the World. Especially for those who are baptized, every candle we light can be a reminder of our own baptism when we first received the Light of Christ from the Easter candle.

> Christ, be our light
> when darkness draws near.
> May we be your light
> for all those in fear.
> Let the light we received
> from godparents' hands
> shine brightly and strong
> throughout all our lands.

Blessing on Birthdays

Both the *Book of Blessings* and the *Catholic Household Blessings and Prayers* have short rites for blessing a person on his or her birthday. These rites may be led by a priest, deacon, or any member of the faithful. The prayer above for lighting candles might be included as part of the prayers used at a birthday celebration.

Forgiveness Rituals

Having a good relationship doesn't mean that there will never be fights, disagreements, or tension. In fact, a good relationship simply means that you know how to fight, disagree, and manage tension in ways that show respect and care for the other. Part of growing in those skills is to practice forgiveness. Just as we explicitly do things that hurt another, we need to explicitly do things to ask for and offer forgiveness.

The church has many practices that help us express sorrow and foster reconciliation. The *Confiteor* is a prayer that we say at Mass at times that expresses our sorrow and need for forgiveness. Other acts of contrition also give us formal words for saying "I'm sorry." The *Catholic Household Blessings and Prayers* also includes prayers in times of family strife and a prayer in time of penance and reconciliation. Be sure to invite your couples to use these prayers especially during penitential seasons in the liturgical year and anytime they find they need to be forgiven in their relationships.

Everyday Prayers

The *Catholic Household Blessings and Prayers* includes a good section on prayers all Catholics should know. These include mealtime prayers and prayers before sleep. Encourage your couples to pray these daily prayers, or others that they might know from their own religious practice, together and separately as a daily habit that helps them grow closer to God and deepen their faith.

Prayers and Blessings for the Days of the Wedding

Couple's Prayer in the Days before the Wedding (based on "Prayer Before Preparing a Family Feast" in Work of Your Hands, *p. 34)*

> Lord, you know all the things that still need to be done—
> the plans and details, the preparation and anticipation,
> the anxiety and worry that everything will be just right.
> As we prepare for this wedding, help us also to prepare
>   ourselves
> that we may not be distracted by all these concerns.
> And when we finally sit down at the wedding banquet,
> amid all our family and friends,
> let us remember that you are there with us
> and that only one thing is needed:
> to love you with all our heart, with all our being,
> with all our strength, and with all our mind,
> and to love our neighbor as ourselves.
>
> Amen.

Gathering Prayer before the Wedding Rehearsal

The wedding rehearsal can be a great opportunity to give the couple's families and friends time to pray for them in an intimate setting. By starting the rehearsal with a substantial period of communal prayer, you can help the participants focus themselves on the spiritual aspects of the wedding and be less stressed about the details of the event. This short ritual might be led by the parish minister who is leading the wedding rehearsal or by the minister who has assisted the couple in their preparation.

The leader might say a few words before the prayer to invite all to participate as they are comfortable doing so and to remind them that the focus of our prayer is on the couple, that they may begin their new life together filled with God's love and grace.

[all stand]

Sign of the Cross

LEADER: In the name of the Father (†), and of the Son, and of the Holy Spirit.

ALL: Amen.

Song

LEADER: Let us sing in praise of God who has gathered us together in his love.

> *Suggested songs:*
> *"For the Beauty of the Earth" (Tune: DIX; text: Pierpont)*
> *"Praise God From Whom All Blessings Flow" (Tune: OLD HUNDREDTH; text: Ken/ Watts)*

Prayer

LEADER: God in heaven, from the rising of the sun to its setting
your name is worthy of all praise.
Come be with us and make sacred this time together.
Come be with us and make sacred our lives together.
Help us remember that your holy presence is with us every day of our lives.
We ask this through Christ our Lord.

ALL: Amen.

[all sit]

Reading   From *Explanation of the Psalms*, Saint Ambrose

LEADER: Let us listen to the words of Saint Ambrose.
We must always meditate on God's wisdom,
keeping it in our hearts and on our lips. . . .
Let us then speak of the Lord Jesus,
for he is wisdom, he is the word, the Word
indeed of God.
Open your lips, and let God's word be heard.
Let us always speak this word.
When we speak about wisdom, we are speaking
of Christ.
When we speak about justice, we are speaking
of Christ.
When we speak about peace, we are speaking
of Christ.
When we speak about truth and life and
redemption, we are speaking of Christ.

Shared Reflection

LEADER: Sisters and brothers,
let us recall the events of these past months in
preparation for this wedding:
the joys and challenges, the hopes and dreams
we have shared,
the moments of true friendship,
and the times when we have needed forgiveness
from one another.

[pause for silent reflection]

Friends, let us open our lips and speak Christ.
Let us bless our friends, N. and N., as they
prepare to be married.

[Invite any who wish to say a few words of blessing for the couple. When all who desire have spoken, invite everyone to stand in a circle around the couple. The parents and the maid of honor and best man might stand by the couple and place their hands on the shoulders of the bride and groom,

while everyone else raises their hands in blessing over the couple as the leader says the following blessing.]

Blessing

LEADER: Love Eternal,
you spoke all creation into being by your word,
and fill every human being with the words of your love.
Help us to be your life-giving word by loving one another,
especially N. and N. as they begin their married life together.
Through their love for one another,
bless our world with your peace,
for you are Father, Son, and Spirit,
who live and reign over all, God, for ever and ever.

ALL: Amen.

[Invite all to share a sign of peace with one another.]

Prayer When Dressing for the Wedding

Gracious God,
you clothe the heavens with the stars
and the lilies of the field with royal splendor.
On this day, let me be clothed with your compassion,
that I may share it with all our family and friends.
Let me be robed in your kindness,
that all might know the beauty of life in you.
Cover me with the joy of your kingdom,
that I may radiate your presence in the world.
And anoint me with the fragrance of Christ,
that your peace may linger in our hearts forever.
This day and every day,
may we always put on love
that perfects the bond we share in you.

Amen.

Rehearsal Dinner/Wedding Reception Meal Prayers

In the *Catholic Household Blessings and Prayers*, part IV, you will find a table prayer that may be used before the meal at the rehearsal dinner or the wedding reception. One of the parents of the bride and groom or a family member may lead the prayer.

The table prayer below also may be used at the rehearsal or wedding reception as well as throughout the year.

"Meal Prayer of Gratitude for Those Who Feed Us" (*adapted from* Work of Your Hands, *p. 58*)

LEADER: Our response to each invocation is "Blessed be God for ever."

LEADER: Blessed are you, Creator God, for providing the rain that waters the earth. *(response)*

Blessed are you, Creator God, for sending the sun that warms the fields. *(response)*

Blessed are you, God of Work, for strengthening the hands that harvest the crops. *(response)*

Blessed are you, God of Work, for guiding the way of those who deliver the yield. *(response)*

Blessed are you, Giver of Life, for inspiring the cooks with imagination and love. *(response)*

Blessed are you, Giver of Life, for feeding us with the love of family and friends. *(response)*

LEADER: We give you thanks, loving God, for all these good gifts

and bless you for the food we are about to receive.

Let the sharing of our lives and the feasting at this table

be a foretaste of the joy of your heavenly banquet.

We ask this through Christ our Lord.

Amen.

Postsacramental Prayers and Blessings

The church's care doesn't end once the wedding is over. Our prayers continue to accompany the newly married couple in the days after their wedding and throughout their lives. Here are some appropriate prayers and blessings that can be celebrated and used after the wedding rite:

- Prayer upon returning from a journey (appropriate for the couple's return from their honeymoon): *Catholic Household Blessings and Prayers*

- Prayer before moving from a home: *Catholic Household Blessings and Prayers*

- Prayer when moving into a new home: *Book of Blessings*; *Catholic Household Blessings and Prayers*

- Blessing on anniversaries: Order of Celebrating Marriage; *Book of Blessings*; *Catholic Household Blessings and Prayers*

"Blessing for Those in Love" (from Work of Your Hands, *p. 66)*

Blessed be the God of Love,
for in love all things came to be.
And blessed be those who live in love,
for they who live in love live in God.
Lord, look with favor on your children
who have shared their love with each other
and thus reveal your presence in the world.

Let them rejoice with those who rejoice
and weep with those who weep
so their love may increase
and extend to all they meet.

When darkness diminishes their delight
and time fades their bliss,
guide them with the radiance of your love
that their promise may be steadfast
and their joy complete.

And when they come to the end of their days,
bring them together to live forever
in the love that has no end,
the love of the Father, Son, and Holy Spirit.

Amen.

11

The Wedding Preparation Team— It's Bigger Than You Think

The Role of the Parish in Wedding Preparation

*I*n the introduction to the RCIA, there is a key statement that the entire parish is responsible for the initiation of those who are seeking Christ (see RCIA, 9). This is obvious if you think about it for a moment. The initiation process is an apprenticeship in the skills required to follow the way of Christ. Who better to teach an apprentice how to follow Christ than those who are actually doing it every day? In fact, it is part of our baptismal commitment to help those who are seeking Christ to find him.

Can the Whole Parish Be Responsible for Marriage Preparation?

Absolutely! The Order of Celebrating Marriage, in fact, says this about the responsibility of the entire parish in the spiritual and liturgical preparation of the engaged couple: "[T]he entire Christian community should cooperate to bear witness to the faith and to be a sign to the world of Christ's love" (26). The way the RCIA involves the parish community in the initiation process of unbaptized adults can be our model. First, we have to ask how we can convince the entire parish to be responsible for marriage preparation. In actual practice, most parishioners do not see themselves as generally responsible for initiation. So far, it has not made sense to them. So how much harder will it be to convince communities that they should be responsible for marriage preparation?

Both initiation preparation and marriage preparation require a paradigm shift, as we have been saying throughout this book. We are not necessarily looking for more parishioners to join the RCIA team or the marriage preparation team (although that would be nice!). What we are looking for is a parish community filled with disciples who live their discipleship out loud. We are asking our parishioners to be much more than just Sunday Catholics. We want them to be living their faith in such a way that it makes a real, measurable difference in their own lives and in the lives of the people they touch.

We realize you have probably been asking them to do that for as long as your parish has existed. The difference we are suggesting—the paradigm shift—is that we are now going to change the reason we ask and the way we ask.

What Should We Be Asking of Parishioners?

The reason we are asking parishioners to be more intentional about their faith is not only for the sake of their own salvation. The way they live their faith is also for the sake of those seeking initiation. And it will be for the sake of those who are committing themselves to each other for a lifetime of sacramental marriage. We are going to raise the consciousness level of our parishioners to help them better realize that their lives are not their own. The way they live, the things they say, the people they are matter to those around them. They have to be or become examples of the faith.

What Should We Be Asking of Ourselves?

However, when we ask for this kind of commitment from our parishioners, we also have to make a commitment. We have to commit to teach them how to do these things. We have to commit to giving them real, doable, *interesting* opportunities for demonstrating their faith. We have to provide them with support systems that are sometimes lacking in today's parishes so that they can become authentic witnesses to the faith. Here are a few things that most parishes can do or do better to support parishioners in their efforts to become better disciples:

- Celebrate engaging, uplifting liturgy, every time, no excuses.
  - That includes powerful, vulnerable, Spirit-filled preaching.
  - It includes singable, spiritual, best-we-can-offer music.

- And it includes hospitality that's not about coffee and do-nuts but about people building intimate relationships with one another, especially the stranger.

- Offer regular, ongoing formation for all adults that strictly ad-heres to sound, proven adult learning principles (see chapter 3).

- Offer regular, ongoing opportunities to talk about and share faith on a deep, heart-changing level.

- Make a commitment to include faith sharing in every parish committee or group meeting and gathering.

- Parish staff and leaders model being people who regularly and often speak about their personal relationship with Christ.

- As a parish community, become a force for change in your neighborhood so that no one within your parish boundaries is hungry, cold, lonely, or afraid.

- End sexism, careerism, paternalism, and clericalism (both lay and ordained) within parish structures.

- Double and then double again your support for the domestic churches.

If we as parish leaders or volunteers can begin to meet these com-mitments, we can credibly ask parishioners to step up to a larger commitment. Once we do ask for that commitment, these are the things we will be asking for regarding marriage preparation. These are based on the role of the community of faith found in paragraph 9 of the RCIA (see chapter 3):

- On a daily basis in their homes—their domestic church—they show the spirit of Christian community so that when they are out in the world, especially at the parish church, they might genuinely be witnesses of that spirit through their words and deeds to newcomers, young adults, and strangers.

- They open their homes and their hearts to engage in personal conversations, in both casual and formal moments, with engaged couples, those discerning a vocation to marriage, and those who are dating.

- They participate in the life of the parish beyond just coming to Mass and invite engaged couples to do the same.

- They commit to making Sunday a priority and fully, consciously, and actively participate in the Sunday liturgy that they may be examples to the children, teens, and young adults around them.

- They sincerely pray for engaged couples in the parish blessings and in their daily prayers.

- They volunteer to assist as greeters or liturgical ministers at weddings in their parish (see also OCM, 28).

- They refrain from gossip and slander; they replace their complaints about others with words of encouragement and gratitude.

- They are attentive to the engaged couples in their midst and look for signs of God's action working in their lives.

- They ask for and offer forgiveness often in their daily relationships; they celebrate and encourage the sacrament of penance and regularly practice the penitential disciplines of prayer, fasting, and almsgiving.

- They make the Triduum and the renewal of their baptismal promises at the Easter Vigil a major priority; they encourage engaged couples who are baptized to take their baptismal promises as seriously as they do.

- They continue to pray for and be genuine friends with newlyweds, and they are unafraid to share with them their own struggles and joys of being married.

- They show compassion to those in struggling marriages and mercy to those whose marriages have ended.

The Role of the Pastor

In the Rite of Christian Initiation of Adults, the role of the pastor is clearly defined. He has "the responsibility of attending to the pastoral and personal care of the catechumens, especially those who seem hesitant and discouraged" (RCIA, 13).

He is also supposed to "provide instruction for the catechumens," "approve the choice of godparents and willingly listen to and help them," and "be diligent in the correct celebration and adaptation of the rites throughout the entire course of Christian initiation" (RCIA, 13). Some pastors choose to provide these ministries directly while others delegate them to someone on the parish staff or to a pastoral team.

The Order of Celebrating Marriage has a similar list of duties for the pastor, not all of which are so easily delegated.

Instruction

First, the pastor is responsible for instructing the faithful "about the meaning of Christian Marriage and about the role of Christian spouses and parents" (OCM, 14). He does this by preaching, catechesis, and "social communication."

This is obviously an ongoing task, and it is therefore in danger of being lost among all the other important tasks a pastor has. In the business world, this is the kind of task that is labeled "important but not urgent." Busy people usually focus on only those things that are urgent, the immediate crises that must be solved today. For a pastor, almost every day is filled with these urgent crises, some of which are not really all that important in the big scheme of things. The challenge is to find some way, no matter what, to carve out time to also focus on the things that are "important but not urgent." These are usually the high-impact strategies that, if attended to, could significantly change the character of a parish. Imagine if the pastor could really think through and create a plan for preaching and catechizing about marriage and the role of spouses and parents throughout the year. How might that change the parish?

Preparing the Couple

The pastor is also responsible for the personal preparation of the engaged couple (see OCM, 14). This is a task that many priests like to do personally, but it is also one that is easily delegated. Perhaps, if a pastor is not finding enough time to attend to the first task above, he might consider handing this second task off to a pastoral team and use his now freed up time to create a preaching and catechesis plan for Christian marriage.

Celebrating Liturgy

The pastor is additionally responsible for the liturgical celebration of the marriage (see OCM, 14). Again, the preparation of this may be something he delegates to the parish liturgist, music director, and wedding coordinator. One thing he cannot delegate, however, is his crucial role in the liturgical formation of engaged couples. This does not mean that he leads classes on liturgy for the couples. Rather, the pastor's best method for forming couples in good liturgical principles, so they can prepare their wedding liturgy according to parish, diocesan, national, and universal guidelines, is by celebrating the Sunday liturgies very well.

Of all the things the pastor will do with the couple throughout their preparation and follow-up, the wedding day will be what they will remember most (and you can bet it will also be on video). The wedding liturgy is the pastor and parish staff's best chance at making a significant impact on the couple, their family, and their friends. The pastor shouldn't pass it off as just another appointment on his calendar, and he shouldn't be tempted to offer a generic homily. If he has invited the couple to genuine faith sharing throughout the process, he will have the content he needs to make *this* homily unique and meaningful for them so they can truly encounter Christ in this liturgy. So the pastor should delegate the things he can give away, and give good focus on this crucial piece of the wedding that only he can do.

Help with Holiness

Finally, the pastor is to help those who are already married so they will be able to make their marriage a sign of holiness (see OCM, 14). This is another "important but not urgent" task that pastors will also need to find time for. However, it is perhaps easily combined with the first task, so that a preaching and catechesis plan could at the same time offer support to married couples and families in the parish. Another way pastors (and all the marriage and wedding staff of the parish) can help with holiness is by heeding what the marriage rite says: In everything they do, they should be "[l]ed by the love of Christ" and do everything in order to "foster and nourish [the couple's] faith" (see OCM, 16). The pastor's attitude, demeanor, and behaviors toward the engaged couple, during their engagement, at the wedding liturgy, and after it, will be the most influential way to show the couple what it means to be holy. No matter how well you preach or teach them about the way of holiness, couples and their families will learn best by your behaviors, especially your behaviors to them and those they love.

Marriage Preparation Coordinator

In the RCIA, there is no mention of a team, a team leader, or an RCIA coordinator. Similarly, in the Order of Celebrating Marriage there is no mention of a marriage preparation coordinator or a preparation team. However, many parishes have found it fruitful to carve out such a ministry. Ideally, the coordinator or preparation team would be given as much authority as possible to relieve the pastor of the bulk of the wedding preparation work.

Using paragraph 14 of the Order of Celebrating Marriage as a guide and by using the guidelines and suggestions in this book, a parish might develop a job description for a wedding preparation coordinator. That description might include the following:

- Coordinate initial interview meetings with engaged couples and discern a formation process tailored for their specific needs.
- Oversee the referral of couples to other staff persons or other pastoral ministers within the parish or those recommended by the diocese, as needed.
- Keep updated on canonical issues, recommended resources, and liturgical policies.
- Recruit, train, and oversee the work of a marriage preparation team that assists with formation of engaged couples.
- Coordinate with the wedding coordinator, music director, other liturgical staff, and office administrator regarding scheduling of weddings.
- Collaborate with the pastor, wedding coordinator, music director, liturgist, and diocesan liturgical staff to develop appropriate wedding guidelines for the parish.
- Oversee the recruitment, training, and work of sponsor couples.
- Coordinate the scheduling, preparation, and facilitation of retreats for engaged couples hosted by the parish.
- Oversee the participation of engaged couples in retreats hosted by outside organizations.
- Facilitate the discernment of readiness of engaged couples in coordination with members of the marriage preparation team, sponsor couples, and pastoral staff.

- Oversee any follow-up with newlyweds, in collaboration with the pastoral staff.

That job description might at first appear to be overwhelming. As we said at the beginning of this chapter, however, we believe that effective preparation for and support of Christian marriage is an all-parish responsibility. So just as in the RCIA, it is not the coordinator's job or the team's job exclusively to prepare a couple for marriage. Primarily, the job of the coordinator is to coach the parish to do its job.

Ambassador of Welcome

We spoke already of the role of these ambassadors in chapter 3. These are your gentle extroverts who are great at networking and drawing people deeper into the "inner circle" of a community. They are not members of the marriage preparation team, per se, but they certainly help the team's goal of getting engaged couples connected with your principle formation resource—the parish community.

Marriage Preparation Catechist

Ideally, you will want someone on your team who knows not only the teaching of the church but also is expert and adept in using adult learning principles (see chapter 3). This person will be able to help your engaged couples understand why the teaching of the church matters in their lives and be able to communicate the teaching in such a way that deepens the couples' love for Christ and the church. This person will also help with mystagogical catechesis after the wedding (see chapter 8).

Sponsor Couples Coordinator

This might become part of the marriage preparation coordinator's job, but it would be best if you had another person or a couple serving in this role. They will know the couples in the parish who would be good sponsor couples. They'll know their stories, their joys and struggles in marriage, and the specific situations they share with potential engaged couples. They would also get to know the engaged couples themselves and serve as a kind of matchmaker between them and the pool of sponsor couples in your parish. This coordinator will also be persistent in asking potential sponsor couples and will be able to prepare, form, and check in with sponsor couples throughout their time of companioning the engaged couples.

Sponsor Couples

The RCIA requires that each catechumen have a sponsor. The sponsors "stand as witnesses to the candidates' moral character, faith, and intention" (RCIA, 10). In the RCIA, a good sponsor really does much more than stand as a witness. Sponsors are companions on the journey with the catechumens, offering them ongoing support and encouragement. We talked about sponsor couples in chapter 6. The support such couples offer might not be as intense as the support an initiation sponsor offers the catechumen, but it could be as significant, nonetheless.

Community Coordinator

In addition to your ambassador of welcome, this person or couple might serve to systematically connect your engaged couples to the activities and groups already happening in your parish that will assist in their formation (see chapters 3 and 4 for ideas on using your parish as the training ground for formation). This coordinator might also assist your couples in signing up for any diocesan retreats or other gatherings that are either required by your diocese for marriage preparation or are recommended resources, such as an Engaged Encounter retreat or a Cursillo.

Office Staff

In chapter 5, we discussed the role of the parish office in welcoming a new couple who want to plan a wedding. Pope Francis also has some advice for this. Early in his papacy, he said in a homily,

> Think of the good Christians, with good will, we think about the parish secretary, a secretary of the parish . . . "Good evening, good morning, the two of us—boyfriend and girlfriend—we want to get married." And instead of saying, "That's great!" They say, "Oh, well, have a seat. If you want the Mass, it costs

a lot. . . ." This, instead of receiving a good welcome—"It is a good thing to get married!"—But instead they get this response: "Do you have the certificate of baptism, all right. . . ." And they find a closed door. When this Christian and that Christian has the ability to open a door, thanking God for this fact of a new marriage . . . We are many times controllers of faith, instead of becoming facilitators of the faith of the people.[2]

Our challenge is to find ways to open a door for couples what want to get married in our parishes. One simple step toward that is a simple technique called "Yes, and . . . " Teach your office staff to never say "no" or "maybe" or "it depends." Instead, teach them to respond to couples' questions with "Yes, and . . . " For example:

Prospective bride: "Can we get married at your church if we are not members?"

Staff person: "Yes, and I'd love to tell you more about our process for becoming parishioners."

There may be some requests that you will never be able to accommodate, but "Yes, and . . . " will work more times than you might imagine. And it will always open rather than close a door.

Another way to open doors is to immediately follow up any request with an e-mail that provides opportunities for keeping the couple connected to the parish. So, for example, you might create an e-mail template similar to the one on the next page. Before you end your initial conversation, ask for an e-mail address so you can send follow-up information. Then, *within an hour* or less of getting the couples' e-mail addresses, add the couples' names to your template and send the e-mail. Each of the bullet points would be a hyperlink to a page on your parish website.

Sample E-mail Follow-Up

[PARISH LOGO]

Dear _____ and _____,

Hi from St. Nicholas Parish. Thanks for getting in touch.

My name is Nick, and I'm the information contact person for St. Nicholas Parish. I'm here to answer any questions you have about getting married at St. Nicholas or anything else you'd like to know about the parish. I thought I'd send you our top tips for finding your way around the parish and discovering who's who.

If you have any questions, just reply to this e-mail. I hope you enjoy checking out some of the links below about our parish. And congratulations on your decision to get married! We are so honored that you have chosen our community to help you during this very important time of your life.

- Wedding procedures at St. Nicholas Parish

- Why marriage is a sacrament

- 10 tips for a great wedding liturgy

- Should we have a wedding with or without a Mass?

People of the parish
- Meet our pastor
- Other helpful staff members
- Couples who were recently married at St. Nicholas

What we do around here
- Young adult Mass
- Theology on Tap
- Parish Festival
- What Do Catholics Believe? discussion group

Get help

If you need any help along the way, preparing for your wedding or participating in the parish, check out these great resources.

- Our parish receptionist (who knows everything and everybody!)
- Our wedding preparation team
- St. Nicholas Parish website
- FAQs about St. Nicholas Parish

Thanks!

Nick

[INSERT CONTACT INFO]

Wedding Coordinator, Liturgist, and Music Director

This may be one person, or it may be two or three different people, depending on your parish's resources. But the bottom line is someone has to be attentive to the liturgical event of the wedding and all that goes into preparing that event, including the rehearsal for the wedding.

In many parishes, the wedding coordinator is not a liturgist but a person who oversees the details of executing the liturgy once it has been prepared by the couple with the priest or liturgist and music director assisting them. What is often lacking, however, is someone who can pay attention to the principles of good liturgy while being attentive to the needs and desires of the couple before them. Usually the priest or deacon leading the wedding will serve that capacity, but it would be best if he could focus on the couple's pastoral needs, including the preparation of the homily, and delegate the details of liturgical preparation to another person.

Honestly, we think we all have to be a little bit better about how liturgy and music happens at weddings. Most of us want liturgy and music at weddings to be the very best it can be. But couples come with their very firm ideas of what makes for the absolutely *perfect* wedding song because they heard it at a friend's wedding or on YouTube or as a twelve-year-old when they were planning their perfect wedding. And why would you be so mean as to deny them their perfect song?

Or maybe it's a poem that they *simply must have* read at their wedding. Or someone must give someone a rose at some point. Or they've been working for months on their own personal vows that say *exactly* what they want to promise to each other.

Many parishes see weddings as an evangelization opportunity. Along with Pope Francis, they want to open more doors than they close. Sometimes we let the principles of good liturgy slide a little so we don't alienate the couples. And who will know, really? Most of the assembly will either not be Catholic or will be made up of Catholics who rarely go to church.

Stick to Your Principles—but Be Nice about It

We sympathize with this notion. But we also want to challenge it just a bit. The thing that makes a Catholic wedding Catholic is the liturgy. It shouldn't look like the latest reality show or a friend's Protestant service. If a Catholic wedding is going to have any chance of evangelizing, it should be the best Catholic liturgy the parish can muster.

What we want to point out here is that someone on the preparation team needs to be the vision keeper for excellent wedding liturgy. That person has to be skilled in using the "Yes, and . . . " technique to communicate an exciting, enticing, it-doesn't-get-any-better-than-this picture of what a wedding liturgy can be like to the engaged couple. And that team member also has to have a bit of a backbone to not want to give in too readily to a couple's preconception of what the perfect wedding looks like.

Oftentimes that person on the team will be the pastor, but not necessarily. It may be that someone in the parish either has been or can be trained to have a very clear and passionate view of how wedding liturgies should be celebrated at your parish. If that's possible, then you will have someone who can help bridge the transition during pastor changes and establish a consistent vision for wedding celebrations in your parish.

Are We Going in the Right Direction?

One last thing to say about this vision keeper. A vision is always something that is only completely realized in the future. The present reality always falls short of the vision. The vision keeper on the team has to realize this and remain both patient and diligent. The measure for success is not, "Are we there yet?" The measure is, "Are we moving in the right direction?"

RCIA Coordinator

Oftentimes, couples preparing for marriage are also in the catechumenate process. If one of the couple is not Catholic, the goal might be for him or her to become Catholic before the wedding. This can be a good thing. The upcoming wedding, the deepening love relationship between the couple, and the challenges of beginning a new life together can all be opportunities and catalysts for conversion.

On the other hand, sometimes the non-Catholic spouse might just be going through hoops to please his or her beloved or in-laws. The commitment to living a Catholic lifestyle might initially be very low.

As we pointed out in chapter 9, there are real and concrete criteria for readiness for initiation, just as there are for marriage. It is important to work with the RCIA coordinator to help the engaged couple reach a point of true readiness for celebrating both the sacraments of initiation and the sacrament of marriage.

One challenge will be the timing of the celebrations. Couples who are not well formed in the faith and have a low level of commitment to a Catholic lifestyle sometimes want to get everything done in time for the wedding. With the help of the RCIA coordinator, you will want to help them discover that they are making a lifetime commitment to a person—the person of Jesus Christ. Just as in their marriage they need to be completely certain about their commitment to each other, they also need to be completely certain about their commitment to Jesus Christ before celebrating initiation. Sometimes they will not be ready to make that commitment before they celebrate their marriage.

Note, however, that sometimes the non-Catholic spouse is already a member of the church. That is, he or she was baptized into another Christian denomination. If the non-Catholic already has a relationship with Jesus Christ and has lived, at least minimally, a Christian lifestyle, the time for his or her formation could be much shorter. The United States National Statutes for the Catechumenate tell us,

Those who have already been baptized in another Church or ecclesial community should not be treated as catechumens or so designated. Their doctrinal and spiritual preparation for reception into full Catholic communion should be determined according to the individual case, that is, it should depend on the extent to which the baptized person has led a Christian life within a community of faith and been appropriately catechized to deepen his or her inner adherence to the Church. (30)

The essential point is that you need to be working closely with the RCIA coordinator and team to be sure your engaged couples are ready to celebrate both their commitment to each other and their commitment to the risen Christ.

Confirmation Coordinator

This person is probably the same as your RCIA coordinator, but the roles are different. According to paragraph 18 of the Order of Celebrating Marriage, Catholics who have not yet been confirmed are to receive confirmation "if this can be done without grave inconvenience" before they are to be married. (Check with your diocese's worship office or tribunal for any specific local guidelines regarding marriage and confirmation.) Therefore, in a similar way that you are working with the RCIA coordinator, you will want to be sure your parish's confirmation coordinator or adult faith formation director is also collaborating with you to assist those couples who may need to be confirmed prior to their wedding. The same principles of discernment for readiness for the sacrament of confirmation apply as we talked about above for those who are unbaptized.

Other Ministers

Prayer Leaders

You may want to look for people on your team who have a natural gift of leading prayer, both scripted and spontaneous. They will be your prayer leaders for your gatherings with couples and on retreats.

Retreat Leaders

Your parish may decide to host your own retreat for engaged couples. If you don't already have someone on your team who is skilled in designing and facilitating retreats, turn to your parish young adult minister or RCIA coordinator for help. They will have experience in leading conversion-focused retreats for adults.

Pray-ers

Continue to connect your couples to those in your parish who can commit to praying for your couples on a daily basis. That's their only "role" on your marriage prep team—to pray for the couples. These may be your daily Mass crowd, the middle-school kids, or your homebound members of your community.

12

Difficult Situations

Cohabitation and Premarital Sex

At the top or near the top of most marriage preparation teams' list of difficult situations is what to do about an engaged couple who is already living together. Some dioceses have very strict policies about this, requiring even couples who have been married by civil authorities—but not yet in the church—to live apart before their wedding. Other dioceses leave this issue to individual pastors and parishes to deal with. So the first thing you need to do is find out what the rules are in your diocese. Read the rest of this section with your bishop's directives in mind.

Conjugal Love

Pope Francis made headlines when, speaking to the clergy of Rome, he said, "Always speak the truth." He then said, "The truth does not exhaust itself in the dogmatic definition" but "in the love and in the fullness of God."[1]

One thing that has characterized Francis's papacy is his emphasis on a hierarchy of truths. Everything the church teaches is true, but some of our truths are more fundamental and require more emphasis. Pope Francis reminds us that we find the fullness of truth in the love of God.

Sex Is Good, Very Good

Sex is an expression of that love. When couples express their love sexually, they are reflecting "the image and likeness of God who is himself love." And not only is sexual love a reflection of God's image and likeness, "[i]t is good, very good, in the Creator's eyes" (*Catechism of the Catholic Church*, 1604).

That's true. But it is also true that this good, very good love is threatened by ego, pride, selfishness, jealousy, sexism, and who knows what else. Sin threatens to destroy the love we express sexually. The bulwark against that threat is marriage. "[M]arriage helps to overcome self-absorption, egoism, pursuit of one's own pleasure, and to open oneself to the other, to mutual aid and to self-giving" (ibid., 1609).

Therefore . . .

- Truth 1: Sexual love is good, very good.
- Truth 2: Sexual love outside of marriage is risky.

Truth 1 is primary. And if we constantly emphasize truth 2, without really saying too much about truth 1, we are getting our priorities skewed.

Couples who are living together totally get truth 1. What is sad is, they don't believe *we* get truth 1, that sex is good, very good. They sometimes think we think sex is bad because we are constantly emphasizing truth 2, that sex outside of marriage is risky.

That is why Pope Francis told that same group of clergy that they should welcome couples who live together: "Sanctity is stronger than scandal," he said. "The problem cannot be reduced to whether" these couples "are allowed to take communion or not because whoever thinks of the problem in these terms doesn't understand the real issue at hand. . . . This is a serious problem regarding the Church's responsibility towards families that are in this situation." The task, he said, is to "find another way, the just way."[2]

Unless your bishop has decided otherwise, we are not sure it is possible to make a blanket statement about requiring cohabitating engaged couples to live apart before marriage. For some couples, a separation might be beneficial. For others, perhaps not so much—especially if they are already raising children together. It seems to us that the "just way" Pope Francis talks about would be to teach the entire truth about sexual love as best we can, giving proper emphasis to the hierarchy of truths in that teaching, and help couples form their own consciences about their response to the teaching.

We should also be careful to make a distinction between cohabitation and sex outside of marriage. For those who are already living together and for whom living apart would not be beneficial, as well as for those who are not living together but are having premarital sex, we can and should advocate abstinence from sex as a means of preparation for marriage and alignment with the Christian way of love.

Annulments

Previous marriage and annulment issues can be one of the thorniest aspects of your ministry. There are often no easy solutions. But here are a few tips to help the process go as smoothly as it can.

Discover Prior Marriages as Soon as Possible

This seems obvious, but you would be surprised how many marriage preparation teams fail to take this first step. Be sure your information form and your initial interview process ask about previous marriages (and how many) for both members of the couple. Also, be clear that it doesn't matter if any of the previous marriages were not in the Catholic Church. Catholics believe that marriage is a permanent bond, no matter where it occurred.

Don't Become a Canon Lawyer

Unless you are the pastor, you do not need to know the complex rules and multiple conditions that make the annulment process such a thicket. You only need to know the church's basic teaching on marriage, which you can find in the *Catechism of the Catholic Church*, paragraphs 1638–42. If you discover a previous marriage issue, set up a meeting with the engaged couple and the pastor. If you are the pastor, you will need to know some basic canon law regarding annulments. However, you still don't need to be an expert. If you run across an unusual or difficult situation, call on the diocesan tribunal for assistance.

Don't Talk about Your Own Annulment

Every annulment case is different. If you or someone on your team has gone through the process, it was either "wonderful" or "horrible." Whatever happened with you is almost surely not what will happen with every engaged couple. Don't give them statistics about the number of successful annulment cases in your parish or diocese. Don't preset their expectations.

Don't Make Any Promises

Along those same lines, don't make any promises about how long the annulment process will take. Don't even imply what *might* happen. Every diocese seems to have a common wisdom about how long annulments take. Let's say that in your diocese, folks believe an annulment process usually takes eighteen months. Don't be tempted to say to the inquirer, "Well, nothing is certain, and I can't make any promises, but the last three annulment cases we had here at St. Dismas took about a year and a half." *Don't say that.* I promise, all the couple will hear is "a year and a half." And then if there is something complex or unusual about that couple's case, it could take longer—or maybe not even be granted. If the couple asks for a time frame, refer them to your pastor. If you are the pastor, use your best judgment about how to reply. If you feel compelled to give a general time estimate, overestimate the time. If the process is completed sooner, your couple will be happier than if it takes longer.

Celebrate the Rite of Acceptance, but Not the Rite of Election

If one of the couple is unbaptized and intending to begin the initiation process, a previous marriage should not usually prevent them from celebrating the Rite of Acceptance. (Again, each diocese might have different rules for this, so check with your chancery office.) Of course, all the other criteria for celebrating the Rite of Acceptance need to be in place (see RCIA, 42). Similarly, for a baptized candidate, there is no reason not to celebrate the Rite of Welcome.

If the annulment has not been granted before the First Sunday of Lent, the catechumen cannot be sent to the Rite of Election. Similarly, a baptized candidate cannot be sent to the Call to Continuing Conversion.

Integrate the Couple into Parish Life

Even before the annulment process is completed, and even if the annulment process does not end favorably for the couple, they should be warmly welcomed and integrated into parish life. Pope Francis wrote,

> Catholic doctrine reminds its divorced members who have re-married that they are not excommunicated—even though they live in a situation on the margin of what indissolubility of marriage and the sacrament of marriage require of them—and they are asked to integrate into the parish life.[3]

Pregnancy

Sometimes as church leaders, we can be too judgmental about couples who are pregnant and unmarried. We have to remember that whatever the church teaches about sex outside of marriage, pregnancy itself is not a sin. We should be as excited as the couple is about the new life that is about to be born out of their love.

It used to be the case that the couples themselves felt embarrassed or ashamed about being pregnant before they were married. We're not sure if that is the case very often anymore. To the extent that it is, however, we need to do our best to provide a safe and loving place of hospitality for them.

And, of course, pregnancy is not, all by itself, a sufficient reason to marry. If the other indicators of readiness for marriage are not present, the ideal situation would be to continue to work with the couple until you and they are sure they will be able to sincerely make their wedding vows to one another.

Different Faiths

Presumably, one of the couple is Catholic or is in the process of becoming Catholic since they are asking to be married in the Catholic Church. If the other person in the couple is not Catholic and has no interest in becoming Catholic, there might be some challenging moments in your preparation process.

Not Interested in Faith

In broad strokes, there are probably two situations you need to consider. In the first instance, the nonreligious person may have no active relationship with God and little or no interest in developing one. In this case, you have a prime opportunity for evangelization. We talked about evangelization in chapter 5. Here we just want to point out the obvious. We don't want to pressure the nonreligious person into any decisions about faith or make him or her feel as though the wedding will be any less esteemed by us because both parties are not Catholic. Most of us get that, and there is probably little or no pressure applied in these situations. On the other hand, we don't want to be *silent* about our faith. If the nonreligious person is in love with his or her fiancé(e), it is at least partly because of the fiancé(e)'s spirituality. If you are "out loud" about your faith, you might spark a flame that could lead to a conversion opportunity.

Active Faith in Another Tradition

The second instance is a non-Catholic who has an active relationship with God, but not in the Catholic Church. He or she may be intending to stay active in his or her faith and may also have disagreements with Catholic teaching. The goal in this case is to help the couple see where they have common ground in their faith and to help them find ways they can share faith together throughout their marriage.

Complex Parental Situations

These days, parents come in all shapes and sizes. A bride might have a dad and a stepdad (or two). A groom might have been raised by two moms and also might have a relationship with his biological father. Or one of the couple might be from a good old-fashioned set of divorced parents who don't get along with each other.

If the bride or groom comes from a loving home, no matter how unusual the parental configuration of that home, our only task in the preparation stage is to help the couple draw on the examples of love they experienced and bring that same love into their own relationship.

When a bride or groom comes from a home that was contentious and did not show many signs of love and forgiveness, the challenge will be to help the couple overcome those negative examples and learn how to live the way of Christian marriage we have been describing.

The real challenge for many marriage preparation teams, however, can arise when planning the liturgy. Specifically, if the couple have their hearts set on a secular-style wedding, there might be some angst over who walks who down the aisle.

The solution is a good-news, bad-news situation. The good news is that no one walks the bride (or groom) down the aisle. Or perhaps everyone does.

In the Order of Celebrating Marriage, the couple processes into the church together as part of the ordinary entrance procession that we experience at any Sunday Mass (with the couple going last, following the priest; see OCM, 45).

The rite also suggests that the couple "may be accompanied as a sign of honor by at least their parents and the two witnesses" (OCM, 46). That "at least" is important here. It means that there can be more—perhaps many more—people accompanying the bride and groom in the opening procession. So all three dads, both moms, and all the bridesmaids and groomsmen can be part of the opening procession.

The bad news is that if the couple imagine the wedding to be "the bride's day" and have their hearts set on a "Here Comes the Bride" type of entrance, they might find themselves less pleased by this pastoral solution than by having to figure out the proper escort for the bride.

Our suggestion is that, as best you are able, you hold fast to the ritual of the church and try in a gentle way to present it as the best option (or perhaps the only option). That might not always be successful, but if the couple has truly gone through a conversion process in their preparation, they will more easily see the value of making their wedding more about Jesus and the church than about themselves.

13

What If We Did This?
What Would Happen?

Big Broad Outcomes

During the papacy of St. John Paul II, bishops from all over the world met to discuss the goals of a Christian family. From their meeting, they came up with four essential roles that a Christian family takes on in today's world. We believe that if we can establish a more sacramentally based marriage preparation process in parishes—one that embodies the conversion principles of the Rite of Christian Initiation of Adults—these goals, listed below, will naturally flow from the marriages we celebrate in our parishes.

Goal 1: Form a Community of Love

A family is not a family without love. This seems so obvious that it almost doesn't need to be said. But we do need to say it because our image of love is so skewed by today's culture. There is, of course, a romantic, thrilling, mind-boggling aspect to love. But once you are mired in the daily slog of paying bills, changing diapers, arguing about taking out the trash, and just plain surviving into the next day, it is important to remember that love is much more a *decision* than it is a feeling.

Love is a gift. And especially in marriage, love is a gift. It is a gift that spouses give to each other, but more than that, it is a gift that originates from the love of God. God gifts us with the Holy Spirit, the Spirit of love, to strengthen us in times when love is difficult. Every day, we call on God's Spirit and God's love to strengthen us. And every day, we get a little stronger and a little better at being a community of love. When we do that, we matter. We matter to each other, of course, but more than that, we matter to the world. The world, which has a pretty messed up view of love sometimes, sees God's love in our Christian families. And the world takes notice. The world begins to see a better way, a stronger love, that doesn't dissolve at the first hardship.

Saint John Paul II said that the Christian family is "a school of deeper humanity" (*Familiaris Consortio* [FC], 21.4; *Gaudium et Spes*, 52). Think about that for a second. When we marry, and when we commit to forming a community of love, we are schooling the rest of the world about what it means to be human. We do this by caring for each other. John Paul II said we do this by caring "for the little ones, the sick, the aged; where there is mutual service every day; when there is a sharing of goods, of joys and of sorrows" (FC, 21.4).

Here's the catch, though. We can only care for each other in this way if we put each other first. We have to give up some of our own comfort and some of our own "ego" to really make this kind of caring happen. We can only do this if we are willing to let a few things slide, give each other a break, and most of all forgive one another. When we form catechumens, we tell them that the essence of being a Christian is that they have to follow the cross. They have to go to the cross. They have to be willing to be one with Christ on the cross. Christian marriage and family makes the same demand. If we are really going to school the world about what it means to be human, we have to start with what it means to be Christ. And that means sacrifice.

Goal 2: Be Life-Giving

The second goal of the Christian family is to give life. Families do this first of all by creating new life, by giving birth to their children. This is at the core of what it means to be human. And it is at the core of what it means to be divine. In Genesis, when the Scripture says we are made in God's image, that's what it means. We create life just as the Creator creates life. And all new life is also created in God's image.

But having children is not the only way we can give life. We also give life when we bring the light of Christ into the deadly circumstances of the world. Whenever we act to free people from death, we are giving life. Death has many faces. It can show up as loneliness, hunger, humiliation, oppression, discrimination, carelessness, and much more. When, as a family, we counteract these deadly conditions, we are giving life.

Another way to say this is that we are moral. When we live and teach values that give life, we are acting morally.

The irony here is that the way to life is through the cross. On the face of it, the crucifixion was a horrifically immoral act. And yet, Christ transformed death into life, showing us how to stand firm in the face of overwhelming immorality. Our purpose as Christians is to follow Christ. And that means we are constantly working to counteract death. That is going to require sacrifice, but it is not an empty sacrifice. Our sacrifice, for the sake of counteracting death, will always lead to new life.

John Paul II said, "In such a context it is understandable that sacrifice cannot be removed from family life, but must in fact be wholeheartedly accepted if the love between husband and wife is to be deepened and become a source of intimate joy" (FC, 34).

So how do we learn to counteract death and live a moral life? We turn again to the RCIA to look at the principle ways we teach catechumens how to live a Christian life:

- The catechumens are gradually introduced into a knowledge of the mystery of salvation through a regular encounter with Christ in his living word and in the teaching of the church.

- The catechumens also learn what it means to be part of the Body of Christ—a community of believers and disciples who support each other and help each other to become more and more like Christ.

- The catechumens learn to worship God and pray to God, especially through the liturgy of the church and the prayer of the domestic church.

- And the catechumens learn how to give witness to the risen Christ—both through their actions in the world and their willingness to say clearly that Christ loves them and loves everyone they encounter (see RCIA, 75).

These four lifestyle disciplines are the framework for living a moral life. These are the four tools we spoke of in chapter 4. In a Christian marriage, spouses help each other to strengthen these disciplines and they raise their children in these disciplines.

John Paul II said that we have an unending opportunity to practice these disciplines as a family. "The Spirit of God . . . opens the eyes of the heart to discover the new needs and sufferings of our society and gives courage for accepting them and responding to them" (FC, 41).

Goal 3: Promote the Greater Good

As Christian families, we are not supposed to shut ourselves off from the world. Our goal is to be active participants in the world, helping strengthen all that is good in God's creation and challenging structures that damage God's creation. The fundamental attitude of spouses, therefore, should be one of hospitality.

This part is difficult, but it is our responsibility, nonetheless. Just as we offer love and support to the members of our family, we are called to offer a similar love to those outside our family who are in need. This is the example Jesus set, and it is the example we follow.

We can do this in lots of ways. We can contribute to charities, we can directly serve in public institutions, we can get involved in political or social welfare organizations—especially those that favor the poor; all of these are ways we can help to make the world a better place.

John Paul II emphasized the role of the Christian family in making the world a better place for the poor: "The Christian family is thus called upon to offer everyone a witness of generous and disinterested dedication to social matters, through a 'preferential option' for the poor and disadvantaged. Therefore, advancing in its following of the Lord by special love for all the poor, it must have special concern for the hungry, the poor, the old, the sick, drug victims and those who have no family" (FC, 47).

Goal 4: Share in the Life and Mission of the Church

The final goal of the Christian family, according to the church, is to be the church. As household churches, we have the same mission as the universal church. And that mission is the mission of Jesus—to announce the good news of salvation.

Jesus, you will remember, was Jewish. And in his day, the Jewish people were familiar with three kinds of leaders. They followed the prophets, who would announce to them the word of God—sometimes in astonishing ways.

They also followed the priests, who offered sacrifice and worship to God in the name of all the Jewish people.

And they followed their temporal leaders—the kings and judges of Israel.

It was natural, then, for the early disciples to see these characteristics of leadership in Jesus. And after Jesus' resurrection, when the early church wanted to baptize new initiates into the mission of Jesus, they identified the newly baptized with the same leadership gifts of Jesus—those of prophet, priest, and king. And still today, when we baptize, we identify the neophyte as a prophet, priest, and king.

Through the love of a Christian husband and wife, these same leadership gifts are established in the family. As families, we participate in the prophetic, priestly, and kingly mission of Jesus Christ and of the church.

Prophetic Mission of the Christian Family:
Faith and Evangelization

We are prophetic when, just as the ancient prophets did, we announce the word of God. That means we have to be in constant listening mode, prepared to always hear God's word in every part of our lives. It is a daily and even hourly discipline.

The marriage preparation process, ideally, will have taught the couple how to attend to God's word in this way. The whole event of preparing for marriage and marrying is a time when our senses are heightened and, for those couples of faith, they are more attuned to hear God's word. As they learn from that experience and try throughout their marriage to stay attuned, they grow stronger in their ability to announce God's word to others.

There are two ways in particular that Christian families do this. And they *must* do this, now more than ever. The world needs to hear from all Christian families right now. We cannot hold back and we cannot be shy.

- First, we have to announce *good, very good* news. God made creation, and it is good. Every person we meet is a creation of God and is good, very good. We can no longer let people stay bound up in their sense of failure or unworthiness. We have to say out loud and loudly, God made you and God loves you.

- That's what's true right now. The next thing we have to do is tell the truth about the future. It gets better. Way better. We have such rich promises ahead of us that every day is a new adventure of hope. As Christian families, we have to say out loud and loudly, God is restoring all things to brand new. We are all being made brand new, and it is going to be so astonishingly awesome on that day when everything is restored. We look forward to that day, and we have to help everyone else look forward to it as well.

Okay, maybe that sounds like fun. It is fun, but maybe it also sounds a little challenging. There is a lot of cynicism out there. Here we are, just one little family. How are we ever going to bring hope to such a jaded world? Well, we don't know if this makes it easier or harder, but we don't have to start with the whole world. Sometimes we can start right within our own family or circle of friends. How many of us know someone who has lost hope, given up, thrown it in? Start there. Bring a little hope to that one person. When we do that, we are being prophetic.

Maybe even that is too hard. Maybe the shell is so thick and the defenses so strong that any good news you try to bring will be rebuffed. That's the reason we have to be such good listeners. We have to listen to how the word of God is coming to us even in difficult situations. We have to stay strong, filled with an inner flame of our own hope and our own faith in Christ. We have to be a light more than a megaphone. Maybe the way we announce God's word isn't with words at all but just by being a sign of hope.

Priestly Mission of the Christian Family: Dialogue with God

Saint John Paul II said that Christian spouses are *consecrated* in their marriage. By that, we think he means that the couples are set apart or designated for a special purpose—just as Jesus was. In a similar way, the Rite of Acceptance, which transforms seekers into catechumens, says the catechumens are also *consecrated*. Both the catechumens and the married couples are consecrated for the same thing: "to sanctify people, to build up the body of Christ, and finally, to give worship to God" (FC, 56).

There is an important thing we have to understand and that we have to help couples understand about the worship of God. God does not need our worship. We aren't doing God any favors by going to Mass or celebrating the sacraments. The purpose of worship is to be united in our *consecration* and extend that consecration to the whole world.

The ancient priests of Israel did this by offering sacrifice in the temple. Offering the sacrifice restored world order and made the world godly again. Christ's sacrifice on the cross ended the need for any further sacrifice. Let that sink in a minute. We say it all the time, and it can wash over us. Take a moment to be astounded! Are we really saying that things are cool between us and God? We don't have to go back and "make good" on all the megatrillions of failures and betrayals we have been guilty of since the time of Adam and Eve? Really?

What if it is really true? If we really believed that, what would we do? We would do what St. Francis did. We'd start singing. We'd do what St. Teresa did. We'd be ecstatic. We'd do what St. Benedict did. We'd make our whole lives a worship to God. This offering of our lives as worship is Sacrifice 2.0. We no longer spill blood. We spill joy. We offer a "sacrifice of praise."

Now, just because we are spilling joy instead of blood does not make our sacrifice any less priestly. In fact, it makes it more so. By offering a sacrifice of praise, we don't have to belong to a special class or worship only in the temple. Jesus has made us all "sacrificers." That is, he has made us all priests.

A fourth-century priest named Tertullian said this about the sacrifice that spouses make:

> How can I ever express the happiness of the marriage that is joined together by the Church, strengthened by an offering, sealed by a blessing, announced by angels and ratified by the Father? . . . How wonderful the bond between two believers with a single hope, a single desire, a single observance, a single

service! They are both brethren and both fellow-servants; there is no separation between them in spirit or flesh; in fact they are truly two in one flesh and where the flesh is one, one is the spirit. (FC, 13)

While this is a joyful image of sacrifice, it is sacrifice nonetheless. Married couples who truly die to their individual egos to become one with each other remind us of the death of Jesus on the cross. Jesus died for our sakes, just as spouses die to themselves for the sake of each other, the sake of their children, and the sake of the world.

In a world that is overwhelmed with ego and selfishness, Christian spouses are a true sign of hope. Their life together is prophetic. By loving, forgiving, sharing, they are living witnesses to everything it means to have new life in Christ.

Royal Mission of the Christian Family: Serve Our Brothers and Sisters

Some of Jesus' followers wanted him to be a king like King David. They wanted a warrior king. Jesus turned the image of kingship upside down by becoming a servant. Instead of having courtiers serve him, he served those who were most in need.

We become king-like when we do the same. Our royal mission is to see the dignity and holiness of every person we encounter. The rules of the kingdom boil down to just two: love God and love your neighbor. If we do those two things, we accomplish the royal mission of our baptism and of our marriage.

When Jesus gave this commandment of love, someone stood up and asked him, "Who is my neighbor?" It wasn't a real question. It was a lawyerly question, intended to narrow down the definition of "neighbor" so we wouldn't have to get too crazy about this neighbor-loving thing. (See Luke 10:25-37.)

Since it wasn't a real question, Jesus didn't give a real answer. Or at least not one the lawyer expected. Instead, Jesus told the story of the Good Samaritan. There is always a risk in reducing Jesus' stories to a single point, but at the very least, the story means this. There is no restriction on who our neighbor is. Everybody is our neighbor. And those who we think might not be our neighbors—the stranger, the "Samaritan," the poor, the weak, and those who suffer or are unjustly treated—are *exactly* the neighbors Jesus was talking about in his story. We might not see them as neighbors at first, but through love we will "discover a fellow human being to be loved and served" (FC, 64.3).

If we just stopped there—if we offered charity and assistance to the needy—we would be doing a good thing. But we would not be doing the royal mission. What makes the mission royal is that we don't see a sick person or a weak person. We see Christ. The person most in need is Christ and is deserving of all the love we have for Christ. So our aid to that person isn't exactly charity. It's more like obligation or justice. What do we owe Christ? Whatever it is, that is what we owe to the stranger on the road in the story of the Good Samaritan.

The Rights of the Christian Family

"The Church openly and strongly defends the rights of the family against the intolerable usurpations of society and the State. In particular, the Synod Fathers mentioned the following rights of the family:

- the right to exist and progress as a family, that is to say, the right of every human being, even if he or she is poor, to found a family and to have adequate means to support it;

- the right to exercise its responsibility regarding the transmission of life and to educate children; family life;

- the right to the intimacy of conjugal and family life;

- the right to the stability of the bond and of the institution of marriage;

- the right to believe in and profess one's faith and to propagate it;

- the right to bring up children in accordance with the family's own traditions and religious and cultural values, with the necessary instruments, means and institutions;

- the right, especially of the poor and the sick, to obtain physical, social, political and economic security;

- the right to housing suitable for living family life in a proper way;

- the right to expression and to representation, either directly or through associations, before the economic, social and cultural public authorities and lower authorities;
- the right to form associations with other families and institutions, in order to fulfill the family's role suitably and expeditiously;
- the right to protect minors by adequate institutions and legislation from harmful drugs, pornography, alcoholism, etc.;
- the right to wholesome recreation of a kind that also fosters family values;
- the right of the elderly to a worthy life and a worthy death;
- the right to emigrate as a family in search of a better life" (FC, 46).

At the beginning of this book we said there are a lot of reasons to get discouraged when we think about helping couples prepare for marriage in the Catholic Church. But there are also a lot of reasons for hope. If, as parish leaders, we can change our mindset about what we are doing when we prepare couples for marriage, we will have reason to hope. If our marriage preparation process seems like a number of sessions that must be attended, can we change it into a conversion process for meeting the risen Christ? If the couples we meet seem like they are just going through the motions, can we change our strategy to focus on evangelization? If it seems like fewer and fewer couples are even asking to be married in our parishes, can we begin transforming our parishes into centers of conversion and holiness so that young people grow up with a clear call to and longing for a life of discipleship in Christ?

The Fire Alarm Is Ringing

Of course, there is a risk to this. When couples come to us without the right attitude or right background or right lifestyle or right level of catechesis, we want them to change. That's natural. But first, we have to change. That's not natural. In fact, that's frightening, to most of us.

Marissa Panigrosso is a survivor of the September 11, 2001, terrorist attack on the World Trade Center. She is a survivor, according to Stephen Grosz, author of *The Examined Life: How We Lose and Find Ourselves*, because she was willing to let go of an old life and step into a new one.

When the first plane hit the north tower, Panigrosso, who was in the south tower, felt the explosion. She also heard the fire alarm go off. She, along with a colleague, immediately headed for the exit stairs. They did not collect their purses, turn off their computers, or make any phone calls to loved ones saying they were okay. In hindsight, this seems like normal, rational behavior. But it did not seem so at the time to hundreds of others who were in the tower. Some people thought it best to first grab their belongings. Some were not even convinced there was an imminent threat and urged others to be calm and wait. Still others carried on as though they experienced a small interruption, like a brief power outage, and continued with scheduled meetings and business.

Not Panigrosso. She and her colleague immediately began walking down ninety-eight flights of stairs, leaving everything behind. But it was too much to let go of for Panigrosso's coworker. The coworker had forgotten to bring the baby pictures of her children she had on her desk. She returned for them. She couldn't risk leaving them behind. It was a fatal choice.

Grosz says of our need to hold on:

> We are vehemently faithful to our own view of the world, our story. We want to know what new story we're stepping into before we exit the old one. We don't want an exit if we don't know exactly where it is going to take us, even—or perhaps especially—in an emergency.[1]

Our parishes are changing rapidly. Old structures and previous pastoral strategies are no longer working. The shift in who and how many come to us to be married in the church is an alarm bell that is sounding.

There is hope. There is a new story that is unfolding for the church and for those we are called to serve. We can meet this challenge because we are, after all, people who believe in the resurrection of the dead. But first we have to be willing to die to the old. We have to be willing to change.

Notes

1 Stop Preparing for Marriage; Start Preparing for Discipleship—pages 1–10

1. *2011 State of Our Unions*, "Social Indicators of Marital Health and Well-Being," http://www.stateofourunions.org/2011/social_indicators.php.

2. Mark M. Gray, "Exclusive analysis: National Catholic marriage rate plummets," *Our Sunday Visitor*, June 15, 2011, https://www.osv.com/TabId/735/ArtMID/13636/ArticleID/3054/.

3. CARA Catholic Poll, http://cara.georgetown.edu/CARAServices/requested churchstats.html.

4. The Pew Forum on Religion & Public Life, "'Nones' on the Rise," October 9, 2012, http://www.pewforum.org/2012/10/09/nones-on-the-rise/.

5. *Evangelii Nuntiandi*, 14.

2 Why Is Conversion Important?—pages 11–23

1. Excerpts from documents of Vatican II are from Austin Flannery, OP, ed., *Vatican Council II: The Basic Sixteen Documents* (Northport, NY: Costello, 1996).

2. Greeting of His Holiness Benedict XVI to the Members of the Pastoral Council, Pastoral Visit to the Parish of St. Felicity and Her Children, Martyrs, March 25, 2007.

3 How Do We Bring Couples to Deeper Conversion?—pages 24–38

1. Charles Arn, "Visitor Assimilation: It's Not Rocket Science," ChurchLeaders .com, http://www.churchleaders.com/?news=138955/.

4 The Four Indispensable Tools of a Successful Marriage Preparation Process—pages 39–68

1. Antonio Spadaro, SJ, "A Big Heart Open to God: The exclusive interview with Pope Francis," *America*, September 30, 2013, http://www.americamagazine .org/pope-interview.

5   Inquiry: How to Start Off on the Right Foot— pages 69–92

1. *Catechism of the Catholic Church*, 2nd ed. (Libreria Editrice Vaticana, 1997).

6   Apprenticeship in Married Life—pages 93–109

1. Congregation for the Clergy, *General Directory for Catechesis* (Washington, DC: United States Conference of Catholic Bishops, 1997).

8   Postsacramental Reflection—pages 122–36

1. *Email Market, 2012–2016*, http://www.radicati.com/wp/wp-content /uploads/2012/10/Email-Market-2012-2016-Executive-Summary.pdf.

2. See Bill Huebsch, ed., *Whole Community Catechesis: Come to the Table* (Orlando: Harcourt, 2006), 54–68.

3. "Christian Initiation in Post-Conciliar Roman Catholicism: A Brief Report," in *Living Water, Sealing Spirit: Readings on Christian Initiation*, ed. Maxwell E. Johnson, 8 (Collegeville, MN: Liturgical Press, 1995).

10   Rituals for Marking Stages—pages 148–68

1. Diana Macalintal, *The Work of Your Hands: Prayers for Ordinary and Extraordinary Moments of Grace* (Collegeville, MN: Liturgical Press, 2014).

2. "Pope: Open the door to faith," *News.VA*, May 25, 2013, http://www .news.va/en/news/pope-open-the-door-to-faith.

12   Difficult Situations—pages 185–91

1. Mark Silk, "Pope Francis gives cohabitation a nod," Spiritual Politics (blog), *Religion News Service*, September 18, 2013, http://marksilk.religionnews. com/2013/09/18/pope-francis-gives-cohabitation-a-nod/.

2. "Francis urges priests not to push cohabitating couples away," *Vatican Insider*, September 16, 2013, http://vaticaninsider.lastampa.it/en/the-vatican /detail/articolo/francesco-francis-francisco-27890/.

3. Jorge Mario Bergoglio and Abraham Skorka, *On Heaven and Earth: Pope Francis on Faith, Family, and the Church in the Twenty-First Century* (New York: Image, 2013), 110.

13   What If We Did This? What Would Happen?—pages 192–202

1. Stephen Grosz, *The Examined Life: How We Lose and Find Ourselves* (New York: W. W. Norton, 2013), 123.